Excel Create and Learn Dynamic Infographic Dashboard Second Edition

Roger F. Silva

Copyright © 2017 by Roger F. Silva

All rights reserved. No part of this publication may be reproduced, distributed, or transmitted in any form or by any means, including photocopying, recording, or other electronic or mechanical methods, without the prior written permission of the publisher, except in the case of brief quotations embodied in critical reviews and certain other non-commercial uses permitted by copyright law. For permission requests, write to the publisher, addressed "Attention: Permissions Coordinator," at the address below.

Roger F. Silva

rogerfsilva01@gmail.com

rogerfsilva.blogspot.com

Table of Contents

1. Introduction 4
2. Downloading the images 8
3. Exercise 1: Line Chart "Sales by Season" 9
4. Exercise 2: Doughnut Chart "Smartphone Users". 19
5. Exercise 3: Funnel Chart "Sales Pipeline". 28
6. Exercise 4: Bar Chart "Customer Satisfaction" 34
7. Preparing your Dynamic Infographic Spreadsheet 47
8. Dynamic Data 54
9. Charts and Objects 62

1. Introduction

Dear Reader,

I have used Microsoft Excel professionally for more than 15 years, teaching and working in multinational companies.

During this period, hundreds of people came to me for help, asked questions and complained about how difficult it was to learn Excel. Whilst looking further into the matter, I observed that the courses and books available were very long, tiring and expensive. People had difficulty learning the "Real-World Excel."

This book is designed for beginners and intermediate level users, to teach how to build a Dynamic Infographic Dashboard using Data Validation, Chart customization, formulas like VLOOKUP, links, and more.

Also, you will have the chance to create four beautiful customized charts through the warm-up exercises in the beginning of the book.

You will follow step-by-step instructions on the creation of a Dashboard, and several customized infographics, rapidly increasing your knowledge. I will not go into deep theories as the purpose of this book is to Create and Learn.

If you want to expand your knowledge of the wonderful tool that is Ms Excel, check out my other publications that are focused on market needs and fast learning.

Thank you for Creating and Learning.

Roger F. Silva

rogerfsilva01@gmail.com

http://rogerfsilva.blogspot.com

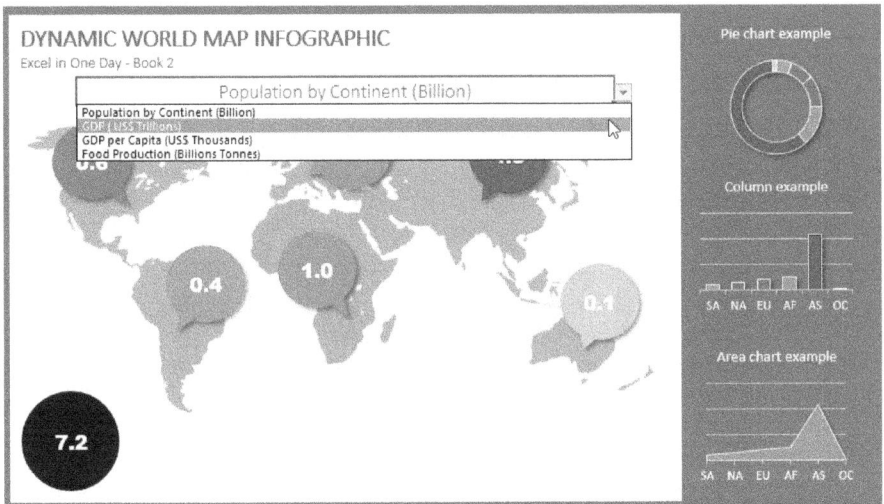

Book subject: Dynamic Infographic.

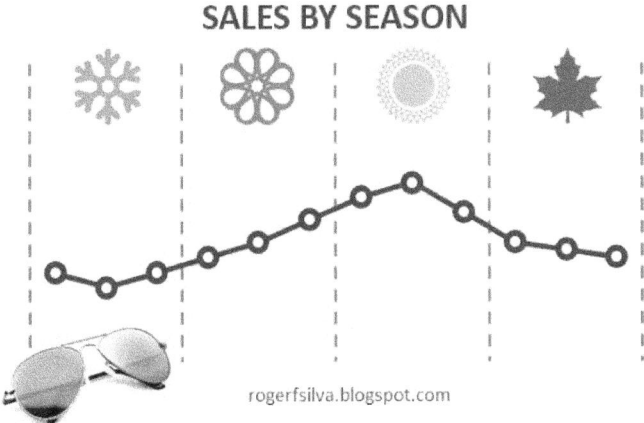

Exercise 1: Line Chart "Sales by Season".

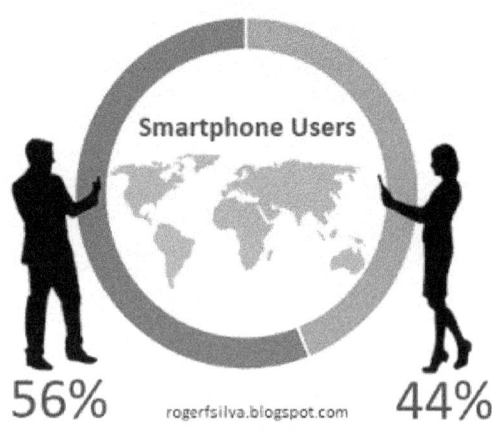

Exercise 2: Doughnut Chart "Smartphone Users"

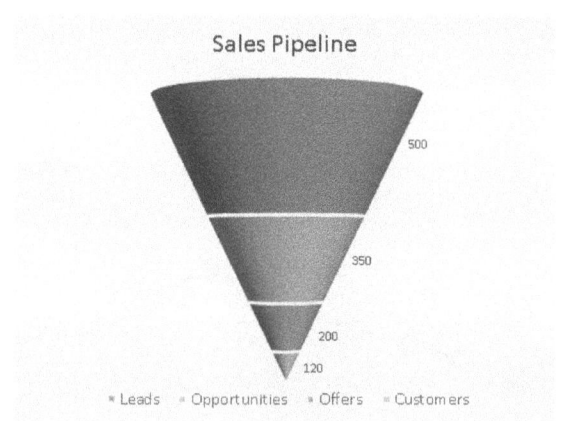

Exercise 3: Funnel Chart "Sales Pipeline"

Exercise 4: Bar Chart "Customer Satisfaction"

2. Downloading the images

You can download the images that will be used in the exercises, and the database table to be used with the Dashboard. If you don't want to use the file with the Dashboard data, there is no problem, you can type the content that is available in the Dashboard chapter.

To Download the content, go to:
http://rogerfsilva.blogspot.com/2017/06/books.html

There you will be able to save the images.

3. Exercise 1: Line Chart "Sales by Season"

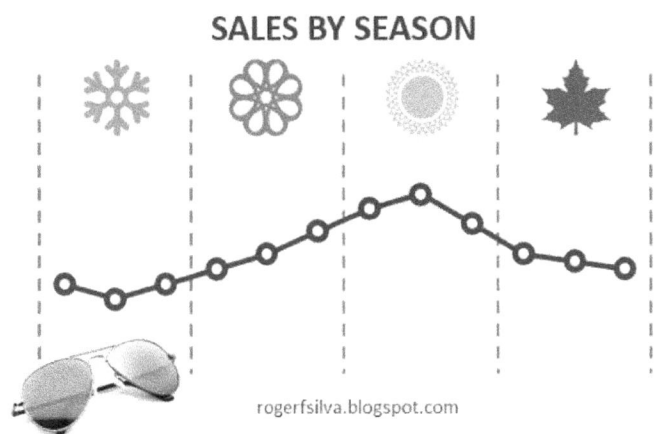

In this warm-up exercise you will be able to create a customized line chart work with images and intermediate level chart configuration.

1- Create a new file and type Jan in cell A1. You will save your time by using the "Auto Fill" feature. In cell A1 move your mouse to the little handle in the bottom-right corner, the mouse handle will turn into a black cross (see picture below).

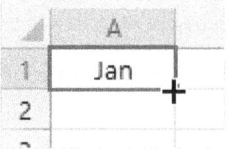

2- Click and drag until L1 to use the "Auto Fill" feature.

	A	B	C	D	E	F	G	H	I	J	K	L
1	Jan	Feb	Mar	Apr	May	Jun	Jul	Aug	Sep	Oct	Nov	Dec
2												

3- Type the values in figure below.

	A	B	C	D	E	F	G	H	I	J	K	L
1	Jan	Feb	Mar	Apr	May	Jun	Jul	Aug	Sep	Oct	Nov	Dec
2	60	50	60	70	80	95	110	120	100	80	75	70

4- Select Range A1:L2. Go to "Home" tab, "Borders" and "All borders.

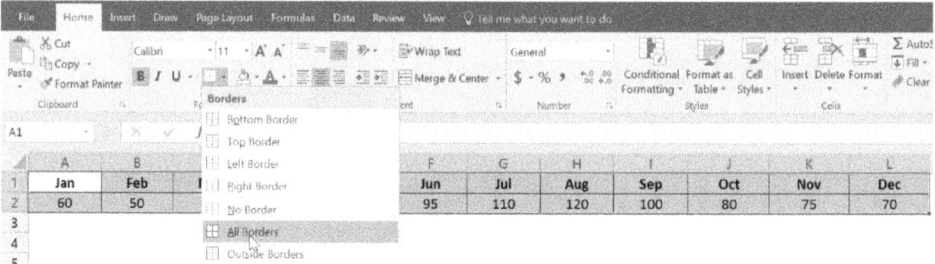

5- Go to "Page Layout'" tab, "Sheet Options" and deselect Gridlines View.

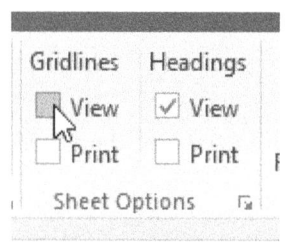

6- Go to "Insert" tab, "Charts" group, "Insert Line Chart" and select "Line with Markers".

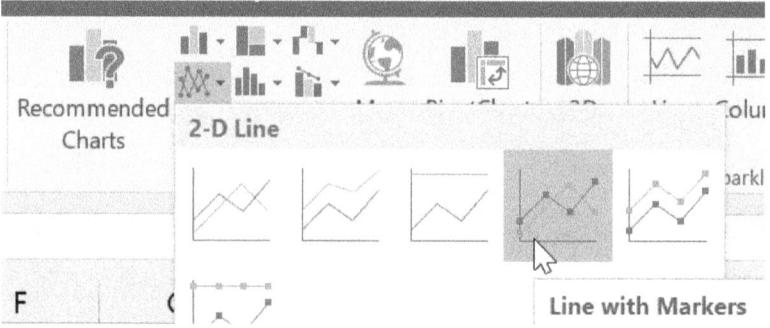

7- Right click the Vertical axis on the chart and select "Format Axis".

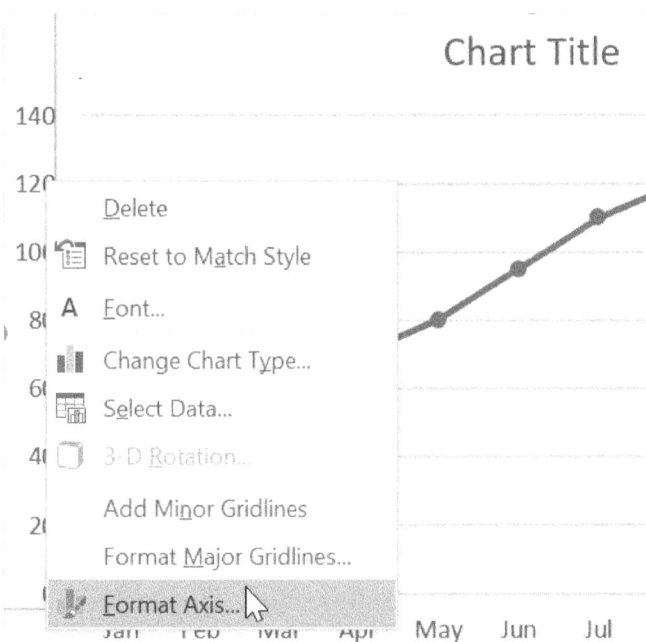

8- Go to "Axis Options", "Bounds" and type Minimum 0 and Maximum 200.

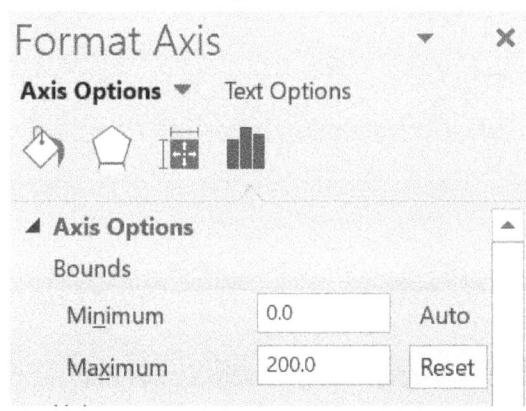

9- Select chart. Go to "Chart Elements", "Gridlines" and check only "Primary major Vertical".

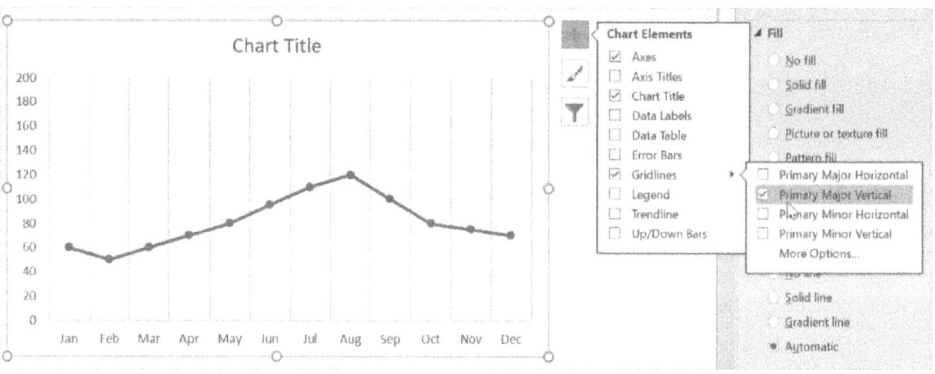

10- Right Click the Horizontal Axis. Go to "Format Axis", "Axis Options", "Tick Marks", "Interval Between Marks" and type 3.

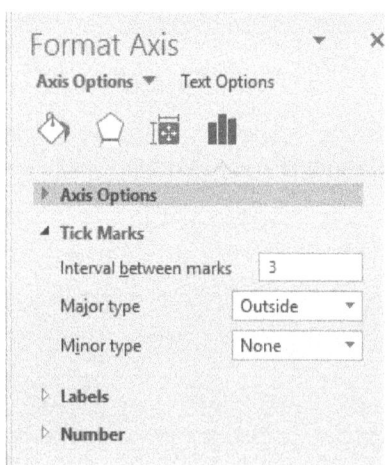

11- Go to "Chart Elements" and Deselect "Axes" or just select axes and press "Delete" key.

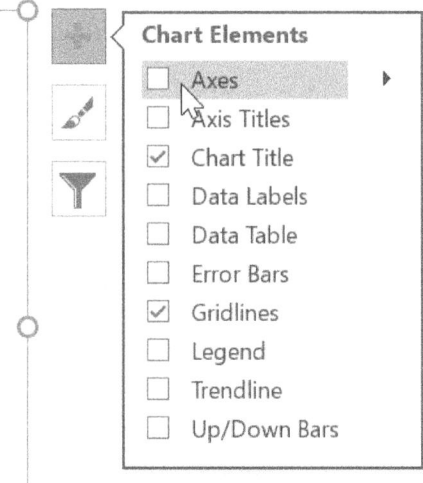

12 - Right click the Chart Series (blue line in the chart) and select "Format Data Series". Go to "Fill & Line", select "Markers" and set as Figure below.

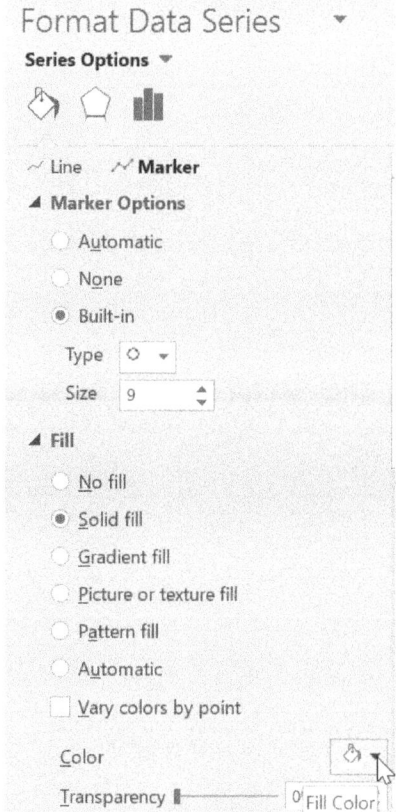

13- Border Color will be "Light Grey, Background 2, Darker 75%" and "Width" 3.25 pt.

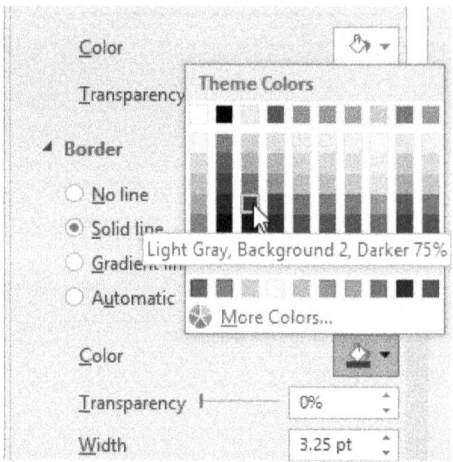

14- Go to Line change the Color to " Light Grey, Background 2, Darker 75%" and "Width" 3.25 pt.

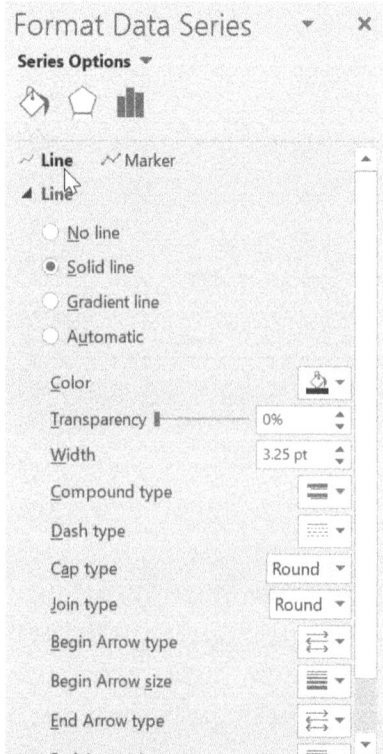

15- Select Axis Major Gridlines and go to "Format Major Gridline", "Line" change color to light gray, width to 1.5 pt and "Dash Type" to Dash.

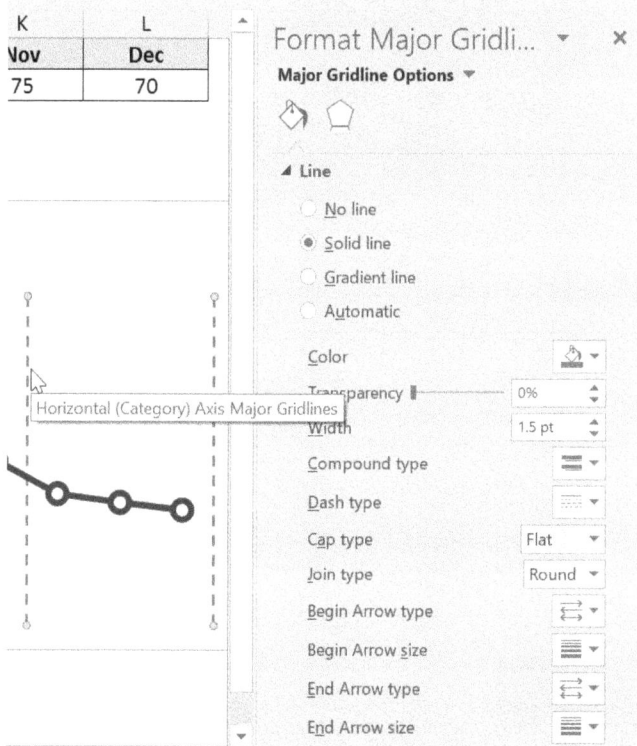

16- Go to the link below and save the five images below by right clicking the image and selecting "Save image as"

http://rogerfsilva.blogspot.com/2017/06/books.html

17- Go to "Insert" tab, "Illustrations" group, click in "Picture" and choose the images that you just saved.

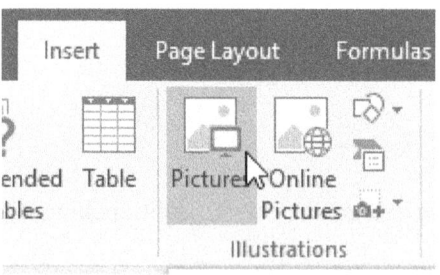

18- For the seasons icons. Go to "Format" tab, "Size" group and set "Height" 1.5 cm.

19- The Sunglasses picture will have "Height" 3.5 cm

20- Select, click and drag the figures to the position as same as figure below.

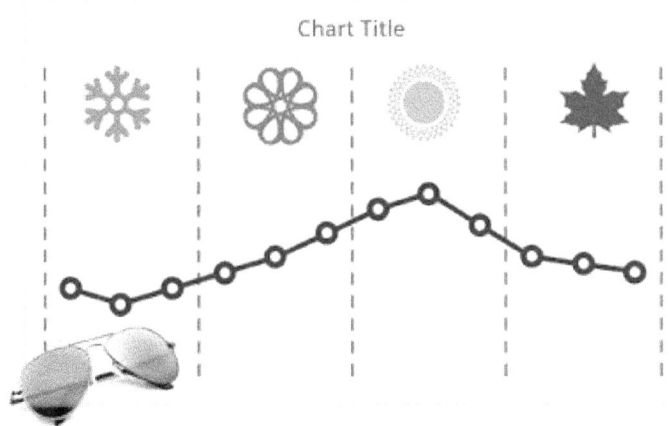

21- Select Chart. Go to "Format Tab", "Shape Styles Group", "Shape Outline" and select "No Outline".

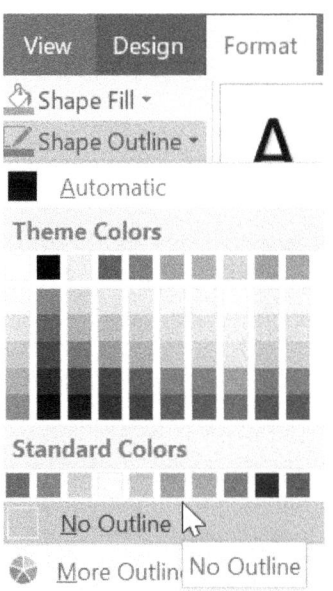

22- At Chart Title, type SALES BY SEASON.

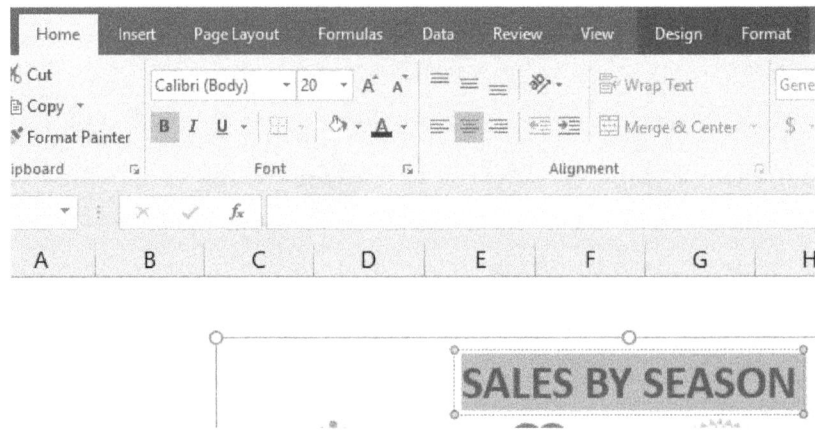

23- Congratulations! You have created a Customized Chart by using advance configuration and figures.

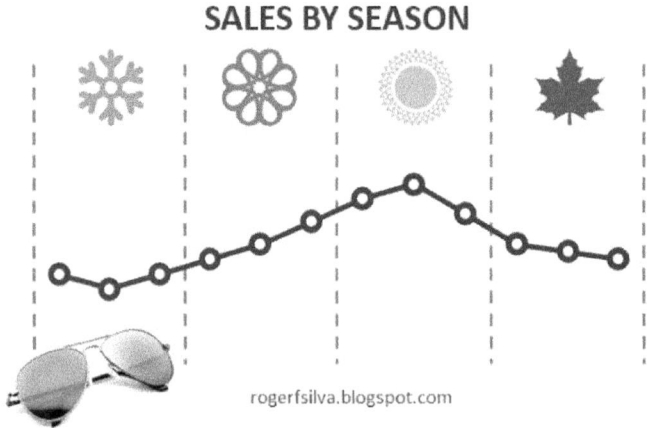

4. Exercise 2: Doughnut Chart "Smartphone Users".

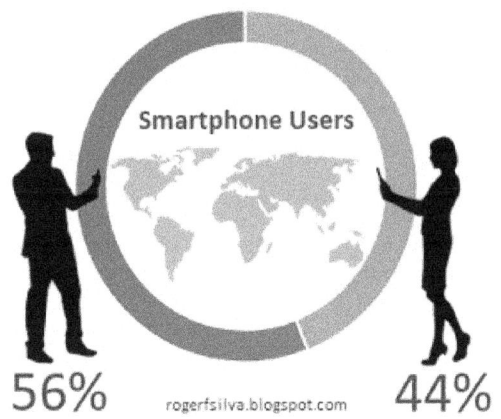

Infographics are great communication tools and have been used through every media available. You can create beautiful Infographics in Excel. In this warm-up exercise you will create a customized doughnut chart and will work with links.

1- Type the words and numbers in Range A1:B2.

	A	B
1	Woman	44%
2	Man	56%
3		

2- Go to "Page Layout'" tab, "Sheet Options" and deselect Gridlines View.

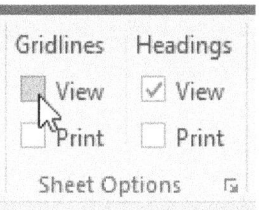

3- Select Range A1:B2. Go to "Insert" tab, "Charts" group and select "Doughnut"

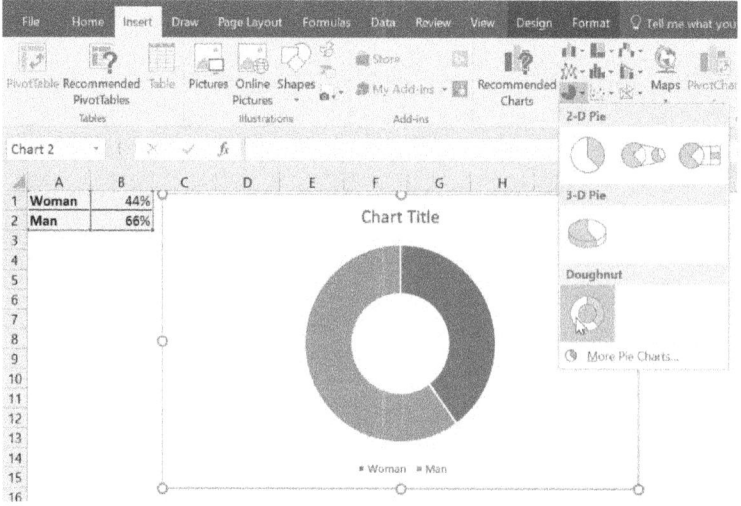

4- Select Legend and press 'Delete" key.

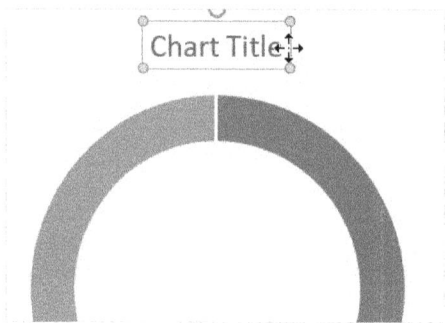

5- Select Chart Title and press "Delete" key

6- Select the chart. Go to "Format" tab, "Shape Fill" and select "No Fill". Go to "Shape Outline" and select "No Outline".

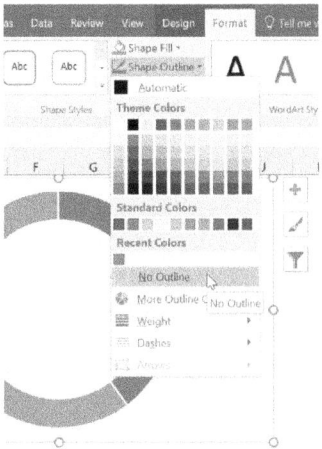

7- Double-click the series "Woman".

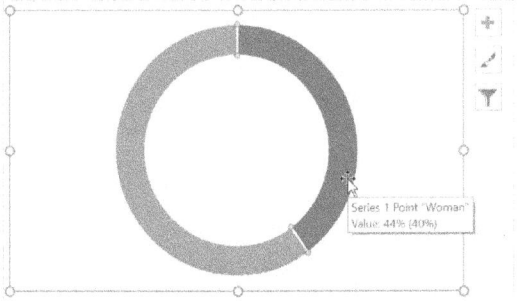

8- Go to "Format" tab, 'Shape Fill", "More Fill Colors" and select Pink color.

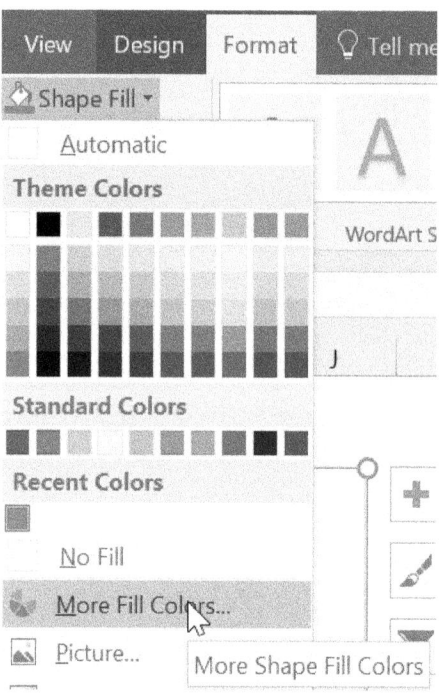

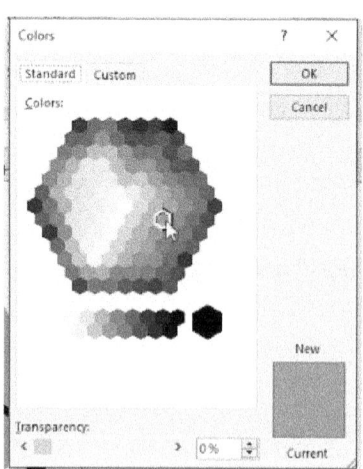

9- Double-Click the series "Man" and select color "Blue, Accent 1, Darker 25%".

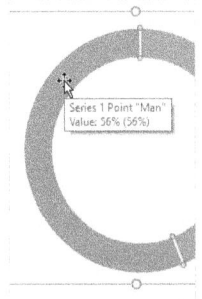

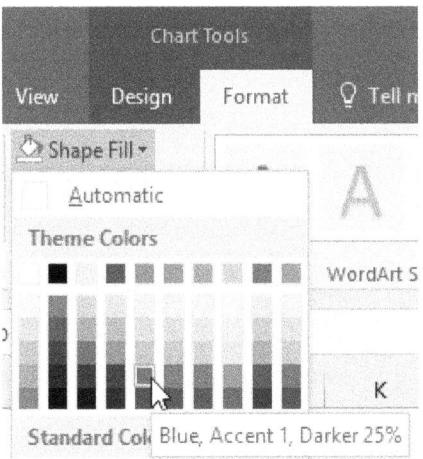

10- With the series selected go to "Format Data Point", "Series Options" and type 81% in Doughnut Hole Size.

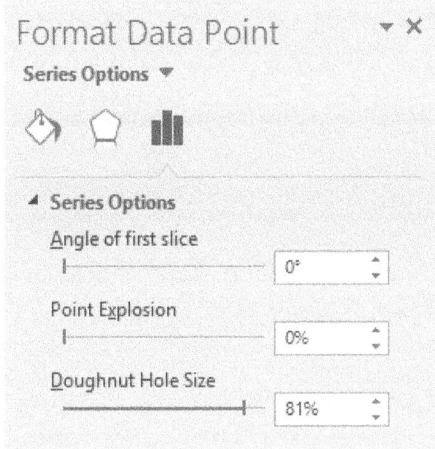

11- Go to "Insert" tab, "Text" group and click on "Text Box".

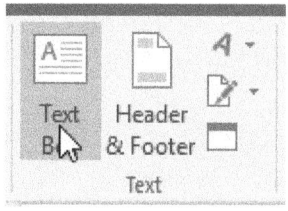

12- Click and drag to draw a Text Box. With the text box selected type in Formula Bar =B1 to link the B1 value into the text box.

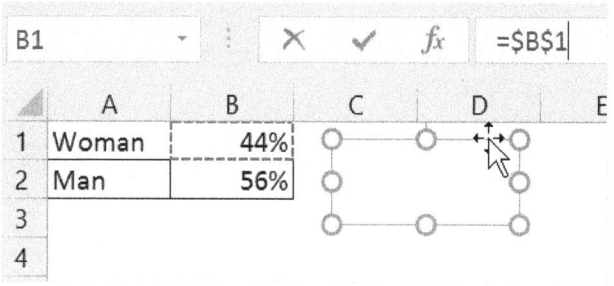

13- Insert a new text box and with it selected type =B2 in the Formula Bar.

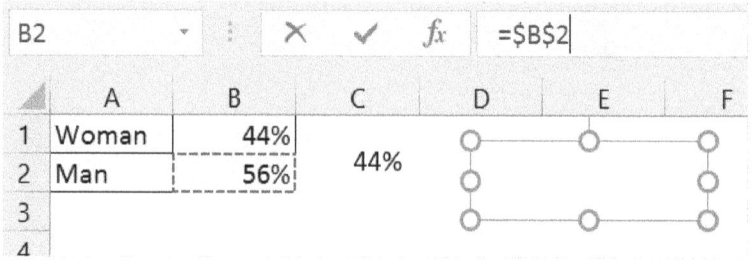

14- Select the text boxes and configure them to "Calibri Font", "Size 32", "Center", "No Shape Outline" and "Black, Text 1, Lighter 25%" color.

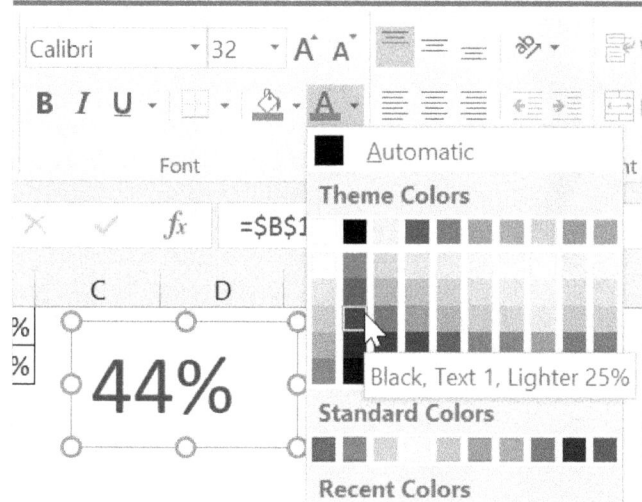

15- Click and drag the text boxes to the bottom.

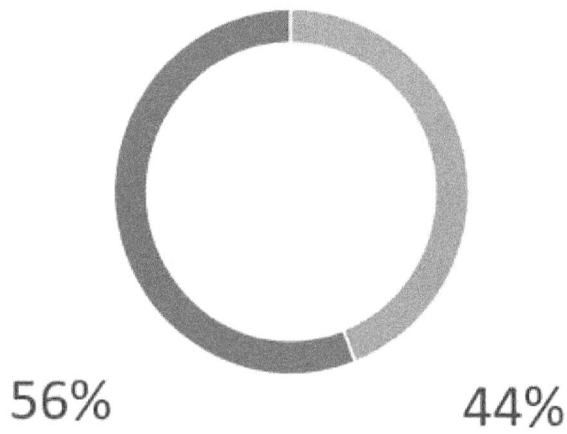

16- Go to the link below and save the 3 images below (Men, Woman and World Map) by right clicking the image and selecting "Save image as".

http://rogerfsilva.blogspot.com/2017/06/books.html

17- Go to "Insert" tab, "Illustrations" group, click in "Picture" and select the images that you just saved.

18- Click, drag the images and re-size them as show in figure below.

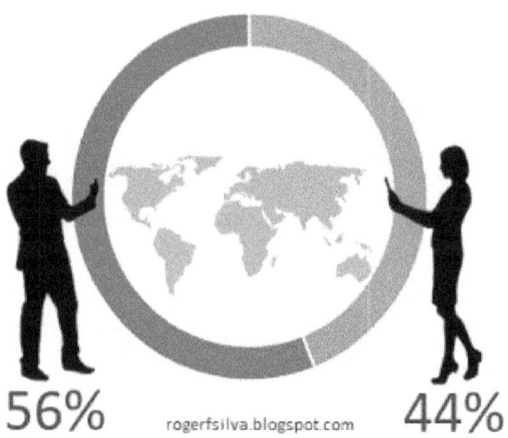

18- Insert a new text box and type "Smartphone Users". Move the text box as show in figure below.

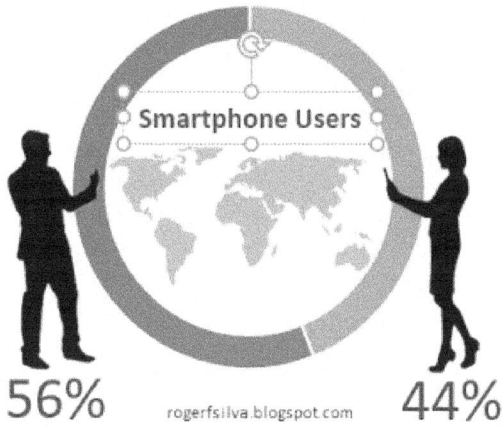

19- Congratulations! In few steps you have created a beautiful Infographic.

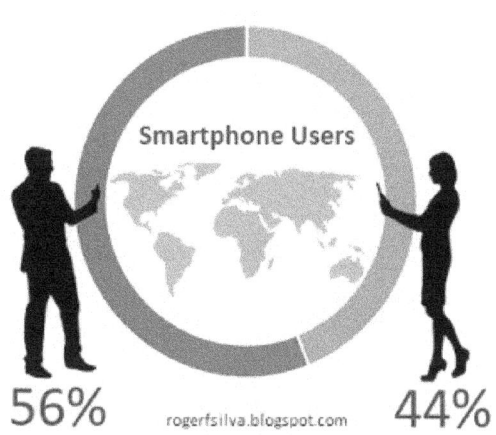

5. Exercise 3: Funnel Chart "Sales Pipeline".

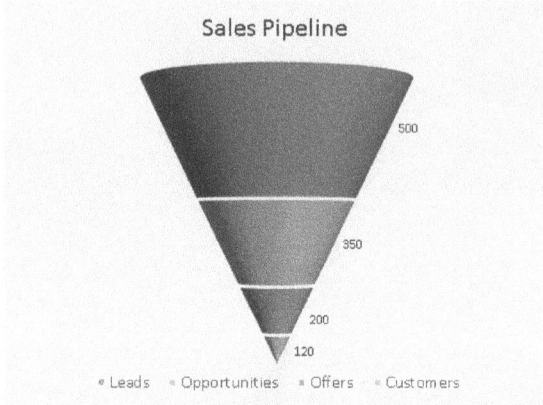

rogerfsilva.blogspot.com

Funnel Chart can be very useful to show stages and proportions in the sales process. Despite its importance, creating a nice Funnel Chart in Excel can be little tricky. In this step-by-step you will be able to create a nice one, following the example below.

1 - Type the data below.

A	B	C	D
	Stage	Quantity	
	Leads	500	
	Opportunities	350	
	Offers	200	
	Customers	120	

2 - With the cells selected Go to "Insert" tab, "Charts" group, 3-D Stacked Column.

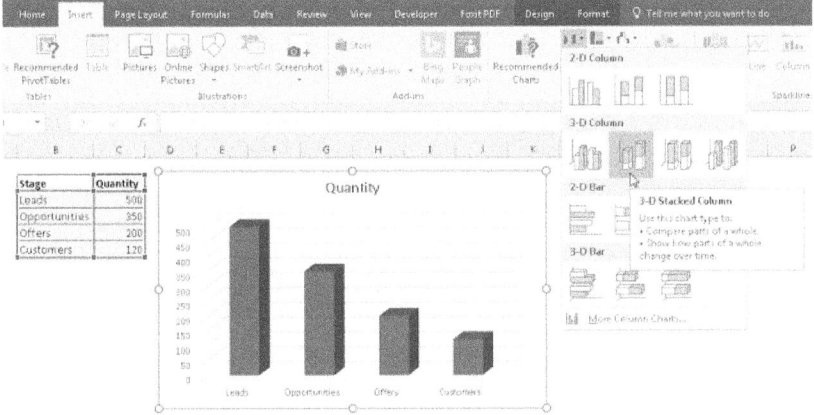

3 - With the chart selected, click in the option "Switch Row/Column".

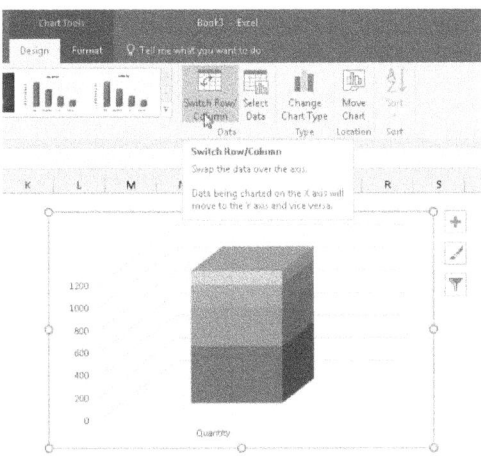

4 - Right click the Vertical axis on the chart and select "Format Chart Area", Select "Effects" and change the "X Rotation" and "Y Rotation" to "0" as the image below.

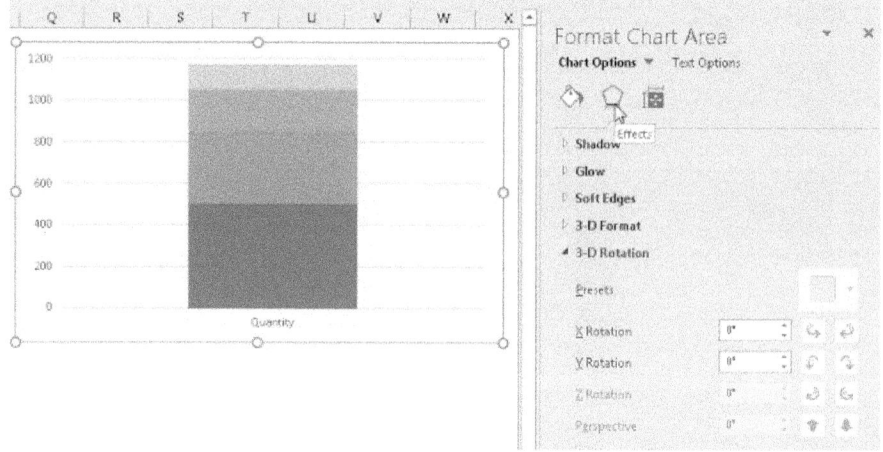

5 - Right Click any Series (bar items) and select "Format Data Series". Go to "Series Options" and set the "Gap Depth" to 150%, "Gap Width" to 80%, and select the "Full Cone" option.

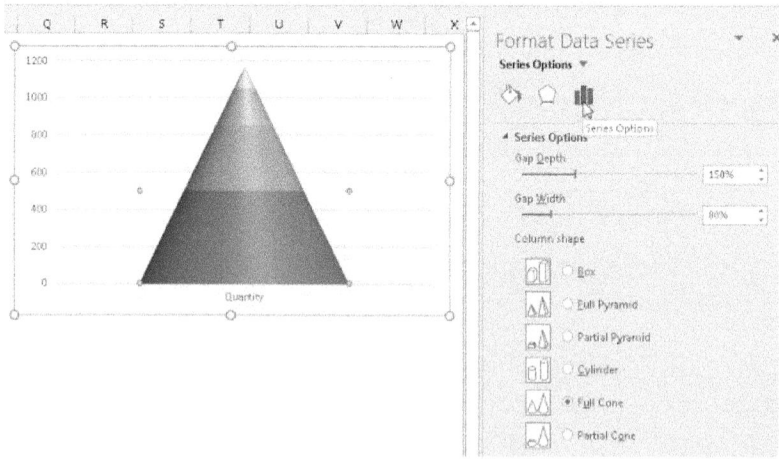

6 - Right click the "Vertical Axis" and select "Format Axis". Go to "Axis Options" and check the option "Values in reverse order".

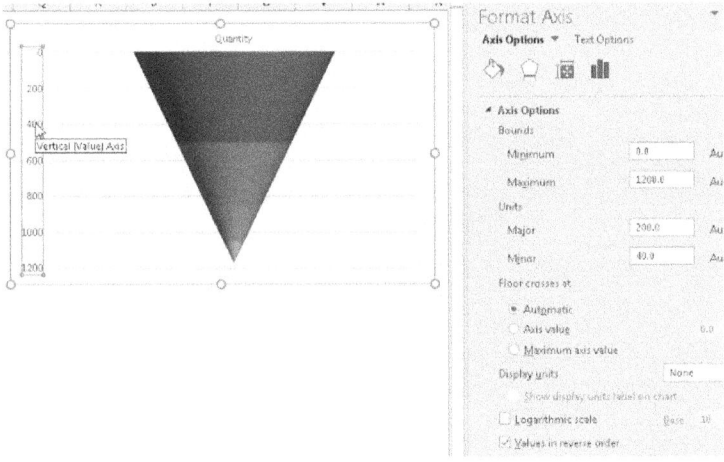

7 - Go to "Chart Elements" and let just the "Legend / Bottom" selected.

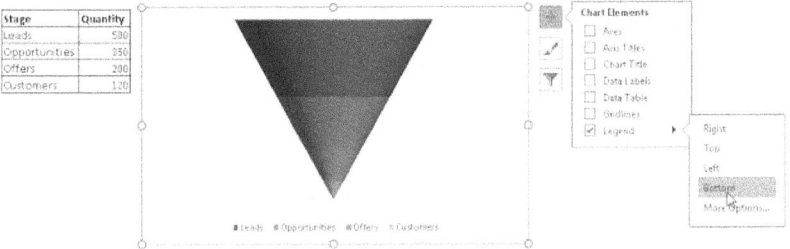

8 - Select the series and change the colors as your preferences.

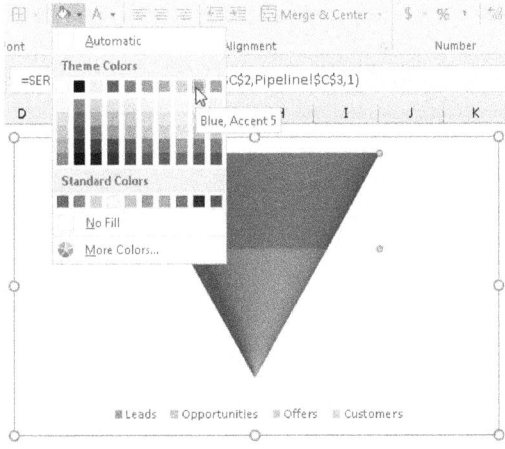

9 - Select each series and change the "Shape Outline" color to light grey and the weight to 3pt.

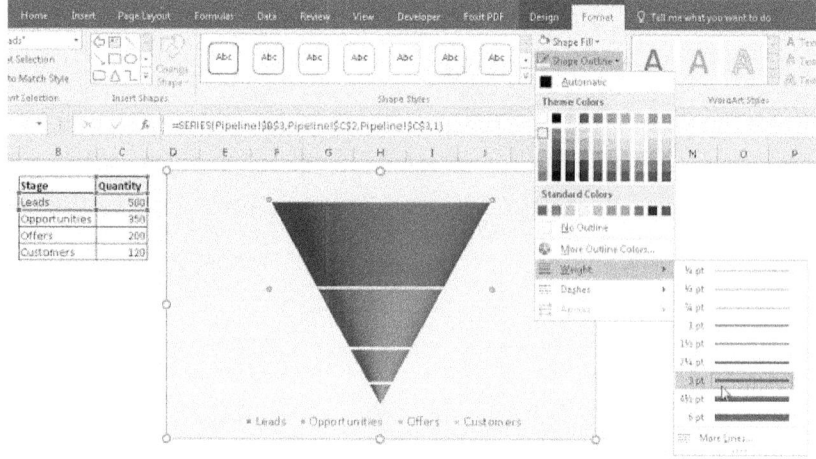

10 - If you want you can insert the "Chart Title" and "Data Labels" as the image below.

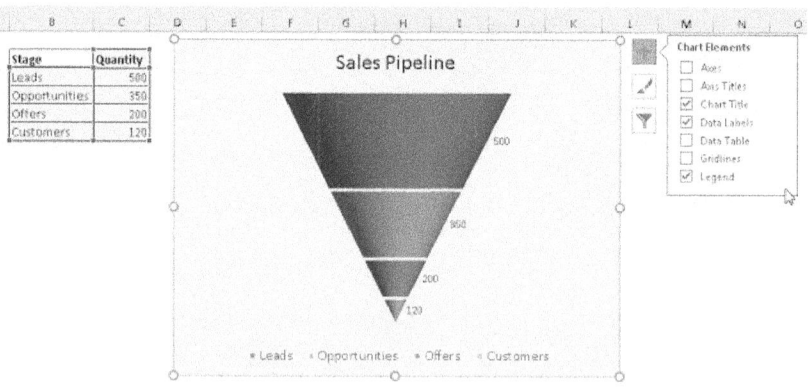

11 - To give it a "Round Edge" effect, go to "Format Chart Area", "Effects", "3-D Rotation" and set the "Perspective" as 15.

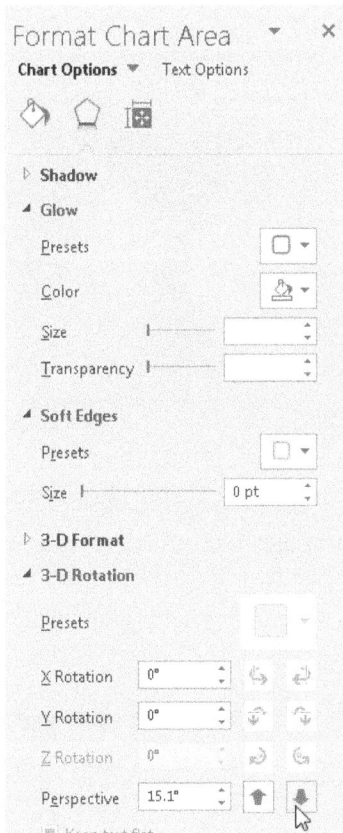

12 - Congratulations! You have created a Customized Funnel Chart! This is a useful, nice and professional look!

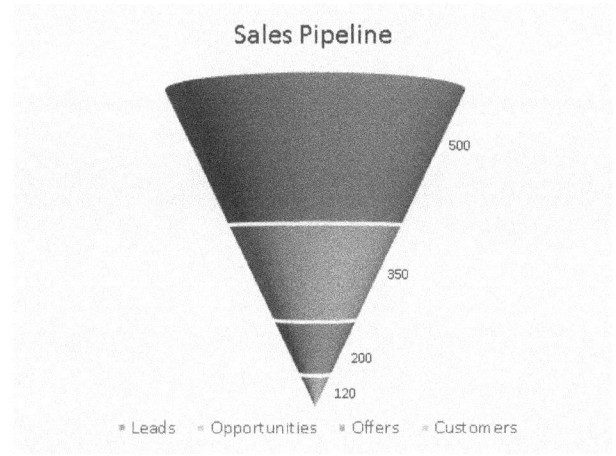

6. Exercise 4: Bar Chart "Customer Satisfaction"

Studies have found that 90% of the information that we remember is based on visual impact. Try this step by step and learn how to use charts and pictures to create great eye-catching information.

1- Type the information words and numbers below in Range M3:N4.

	L	M	N
1			
2			
3		Men	100%
4		Women	100%

2- Type CUSTOMER SATISFACTION in cell A1.

	A	B	C
1	CUSTOMER SATISFACTION		
2			

3- Select Range A3:K20. Go to "Home" tab, "Font" group, "Fill Color" and select Gray 25%.

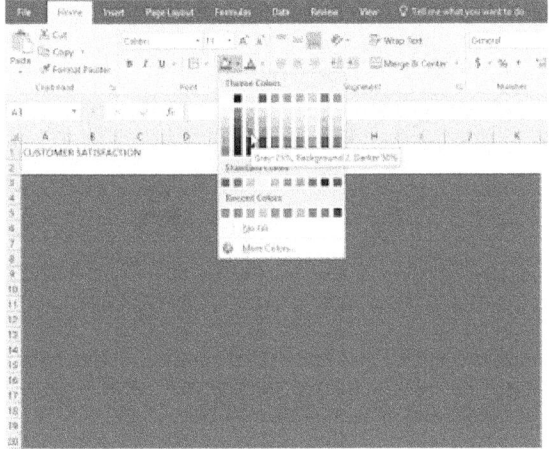

4- Go to "Insert" tab, "Illustrations" group, click on "Shapes" and select "Oval". Click and drag to create a circle.

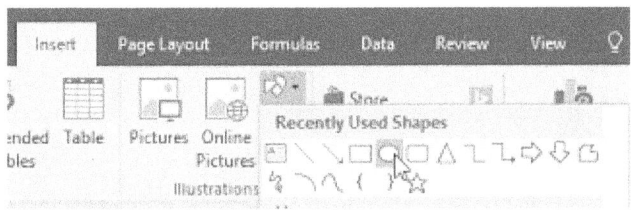

5- Go to "Format" tab, "Size" group and set the "Height" and "Width" to 8cm.

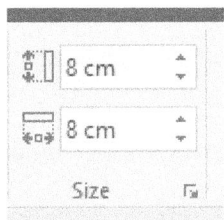

6- Go to "Format" tab, "Shape Outline" and select "No outline".

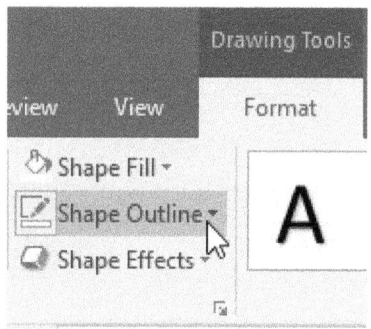

7- Copy and paste the shape and drag as figure below.

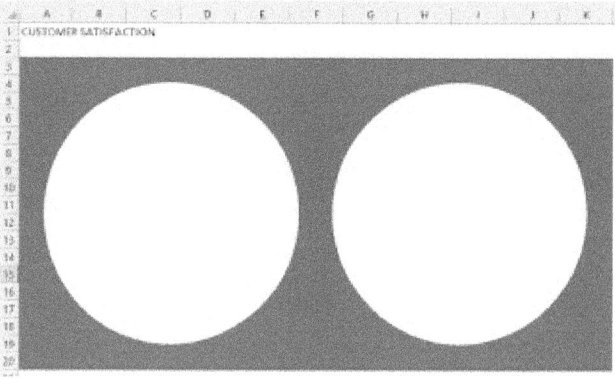

8- Select Range M3:N3. Go to "Insert" tab, "Charts" group, "Insert Column Bar" and select clustered column.

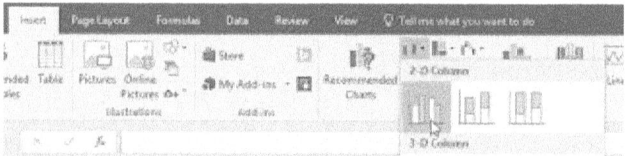

9- Right click the vertical Axis and select "Format Axis".

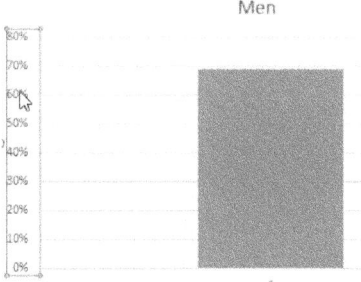

10- Go to "Axis Options", "Maximum" and type 1.0. "Minimum" and Type 0.0.

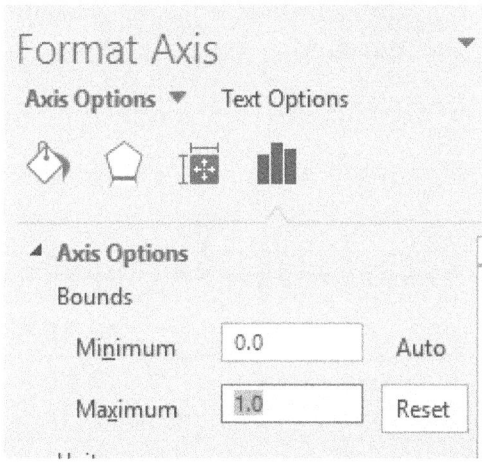

11- Delete the Axis, Titles, Legend and Gridlines.

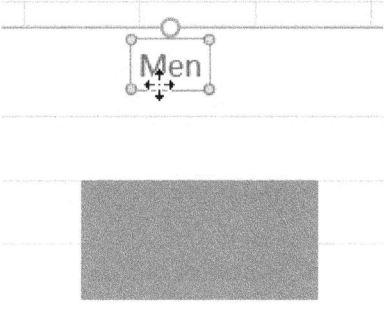

12- You can press "Delete" key or use the "Chart Elements" box.

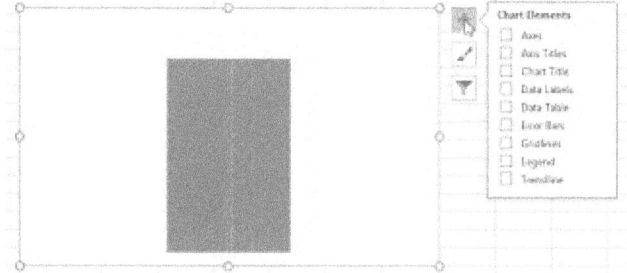

13- With the chart selected format "No Outline" and "No Fill",

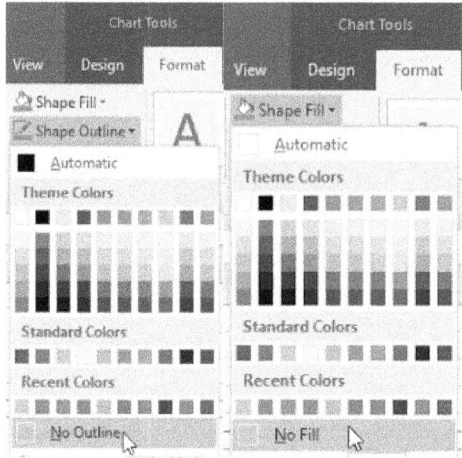

14- Go to "Page Layout'" tab, "Sheet Options" and deselect Gridlines View.

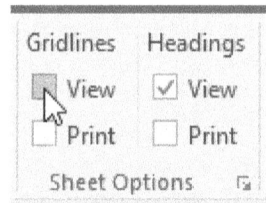

15- Double click the Series "Men", right click and select "Format Data Point".

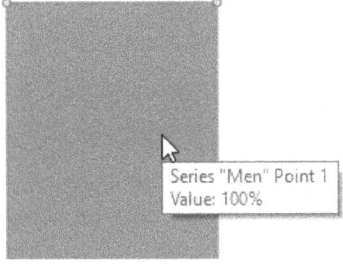

16- Go to "Series Options", "Gap Width" and type 0%.

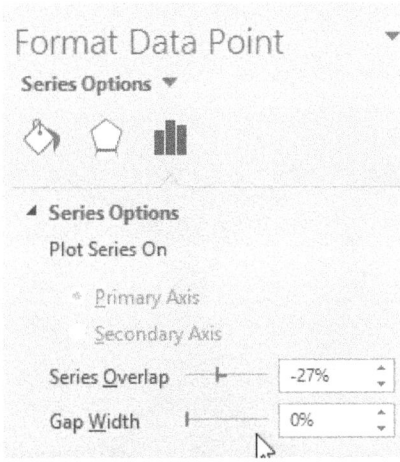

17- Go to "Format" tab, "Size" group and set "Height" 6.5cm and "Width" 2.5cm

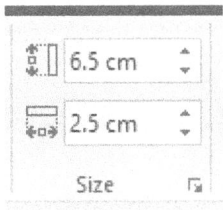

18- Go to "Shape Fill" and select "Gold, Accent 4" color.

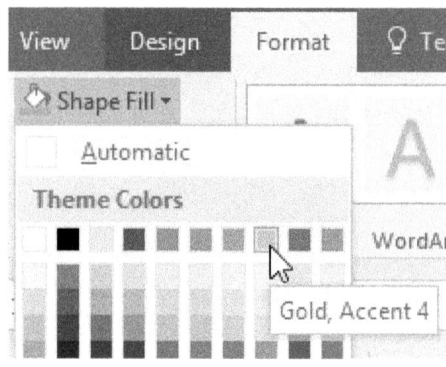

19- Copy the chart, select cell G4 and paste.

20- Click and drag the charts.

21- Select Right Chart, and change the data to Range M4:N4.

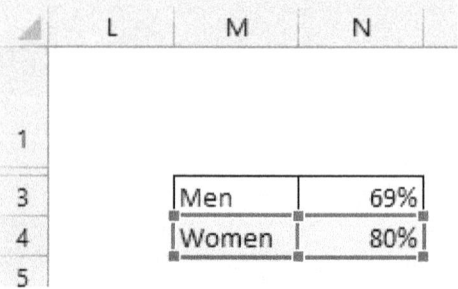

22- Double click the chart on Series "Woman". Go to "Shape Fill" and "More Fill

Colors". Select as figure below.

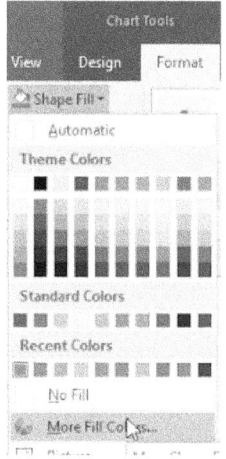

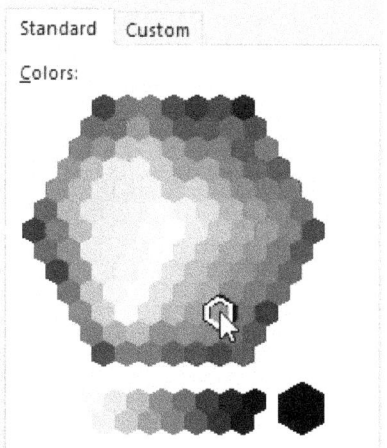

23- Your spreadsheet should be like this:

24- Remember that you can select the shapes or charts and Bring Forward or Send Backward by using the option below.

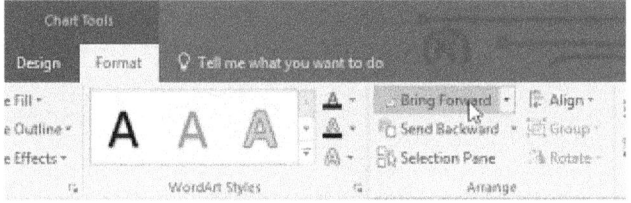

25- Go to the link below and save the image below (Man and Woman) by right clicking the image and selecting "Save image as".

http://rogerfsilva.blogspot.com/2017/06/books.html

26- Go to "Insert" tab, "Illustrations" group, click in "Picture" and choose the images that you just saved.

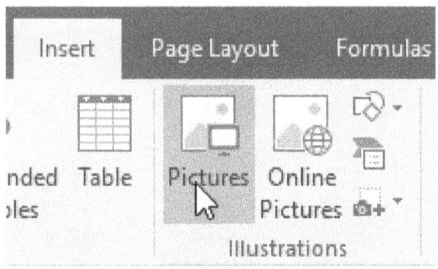

27- Change their Heights to 6.25cm.

28- Click and drag the images over the charts. Change the values to 69% and 80%.

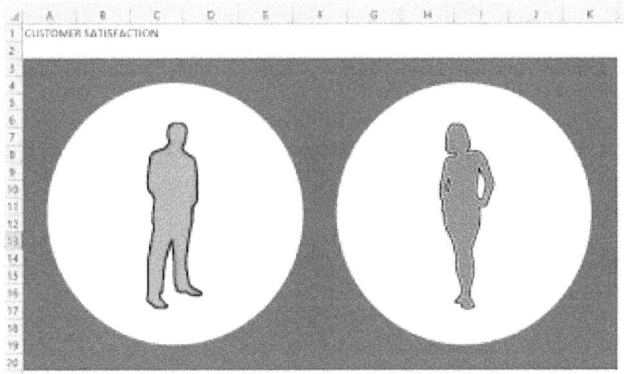

29- Go to "Insert" tab, "Text" group and click on "Text Box".

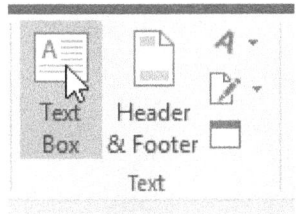

30- Click and drag to draw a Text Box. With the text box selected type in Formula Bar =N3 to link the N3 value into the text box.

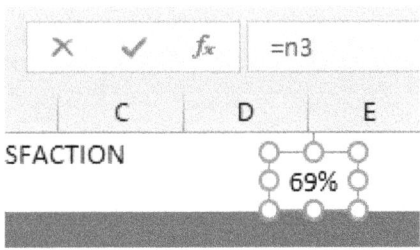

31- Create one more text box. Click and drag to draw a Text Box. With the text box selected type in Formula Bar =N4 to link the N4 value into the text box.

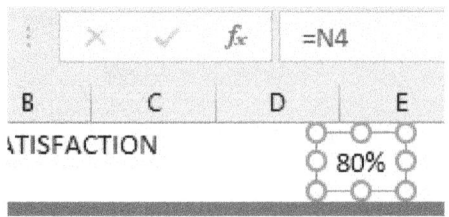

32- Configure each text box as image below. "Forte Font", "Size 28", and colors. Click and drag them.

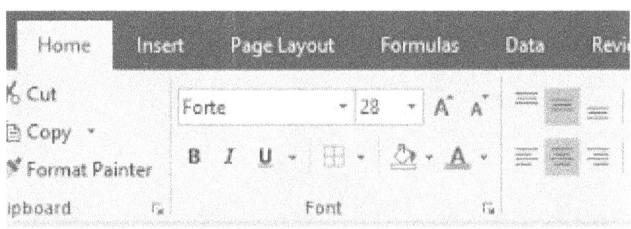

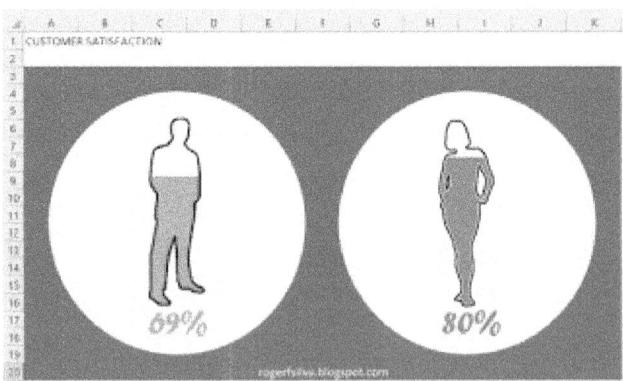

33-Select Range A1:K1. Go to "Home" tab, "Alignment" group and select "Merge & Center".

34- Configure the Range as image below. "Eras Bold Font", "Size 26", "Font Color White", " Fill Color, Gray -25%, Darker 75%", "Bottom Align" and "Center".

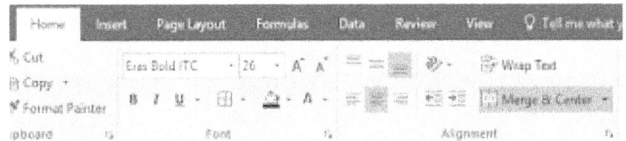

35- Change Row1 height to 45.

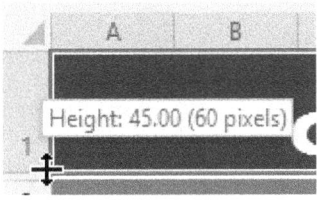

36- Change Row2 height to 3.

37- Change Row 21 height to 3.

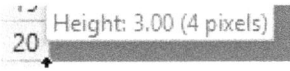

38- Select Range A22:K22 and change color.

39- Change Row 22 height to 7.50.

40- Congratulations! You have used Chart and Pictures to create an Eye-Catching Information.

7. Preparing your Dynamic Infographic Spreadsheet

Before anything else, preparation is the key to success.

- Alexander Graham Bell, scientist, inventor, engineer and innovator.

In this chapter you will prepare your spreadsheet and use different formatting. If you have any questions throughout the book you may use overview video available on the internet (see the video URL on the last chapter of this book).

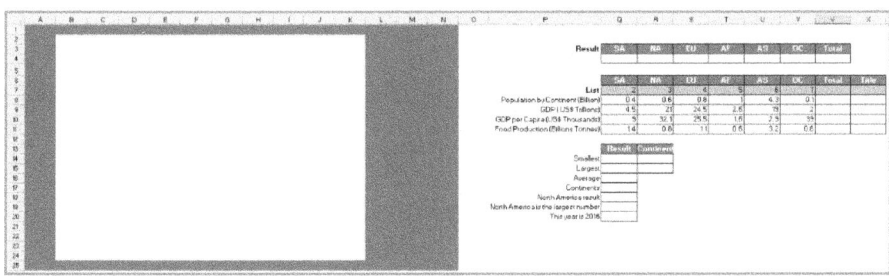

Example 1

1. Let's start by finding the Excel application and opening it.

2. At the desktop environment click on the option "Blank workbook".

3. Your file will already be named, possibly as "Book1".

4. Rename it by clicking on "File" and then the left option "Save".

5. Excel will show you many options to save your file. Choose "Browse" option.

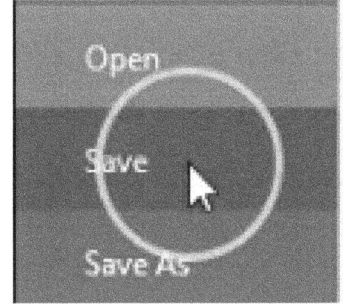

6. The "Save popup" will appear and you can select the location you wish to save the file. Type the name Create and Learn – Dynamic Infographic.xlsx and click "OK" or press "Enter" in your keyboard.

7. Fill Range P3:W4 with the data below (don't use space).

	P	Q	R	S	T	U	V	W
3	Result	SA	NA	EU	AF	AS	OC	Total

8. Fill Range P6:X11 with the data below.

	P	Q	R	S	T	U	V	W	X
6		SA	NA	EU	AF	AS	OC	Total	Title
7	List								
8	Population by Continent (Billion)								
9	GDP (US$ Trillions)								
10	GDP per Capita (US$ Thousands)								
11	Food Production (Billions Tonnes)								

9. Fill the Range P13:R20 with the data below.

	P	Q	R	S
13		Result	Continent	
14	Smallest			
15	Largest			
16	Average			
17	Continents			
18	North America result			
19	North America is the largest number			
20	This year is 2016			

10. Select Range Q3:W4. You can click in cell Q3, hold Shift Key, click in cell W4 and release the Shift Key or Click in cell Q3 and drag until cell W4.

	P	Q	R	S	T	U	V	W
3	Result	SA	NA	EU	AF	AS	OC	Total
4								

11. Go to the "Home Tab", "Font group", click on "Border" and select "All borders".

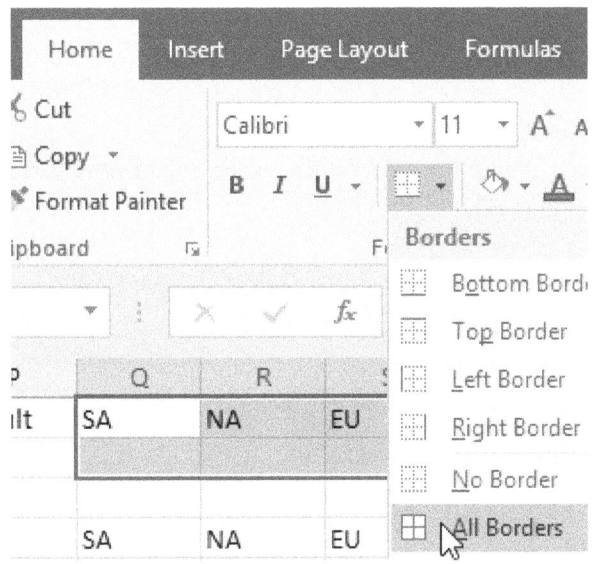

12. Select Range Q6:X11 and go to the "Home Tab", "Font group", click on "Border" and select "All borders".

13. Select Range Q13:Q20, hold "Crtl" and select range R13:R15. Then go to the "Home Tab", "Font group", click on "Border" and select "All borders".

14. Move your mouse between Column P and Column Q. Double click to expand column P

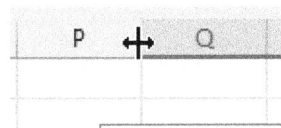

15. Select Column Range Q:X.

16. Click column Q with the right button, select the "Column Width" option, configure the width to 10 and click "OK".

17. Go to the "Page Layout Tab", then "Sheet Options Group" and uncheck "Gridlines View".

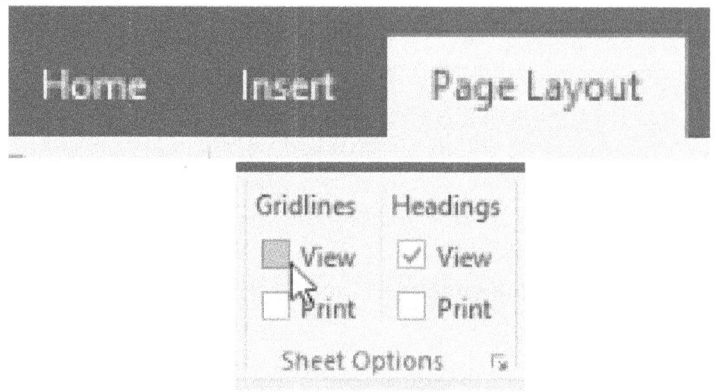

18. Select Range Q3:W3, then go to the "Home Tab", "Font group" and then click on "Fill Color" and choose "Gray -25%, Background 2, Darker 50%" or another Grey color if you have a different Excel version.

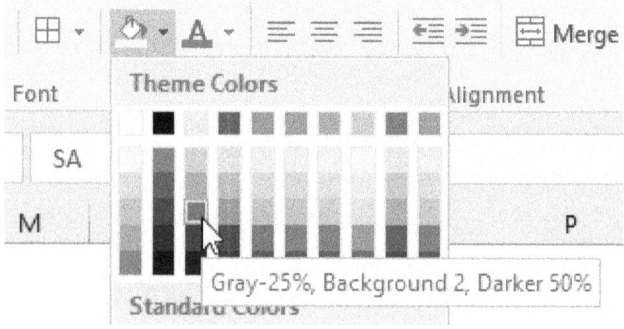

19. With the range selected, go to the "Home Tab", "Alignment group" and click on "Center".

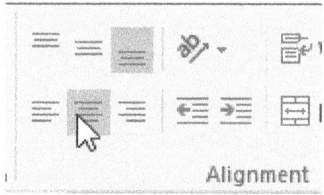

20. With the range selected, go to the "Home Tab", "Font group" and click on "Bold".

21. Go to the "Home Tab", "Font group" and click on "Font Color" then choose "White, Background 1".

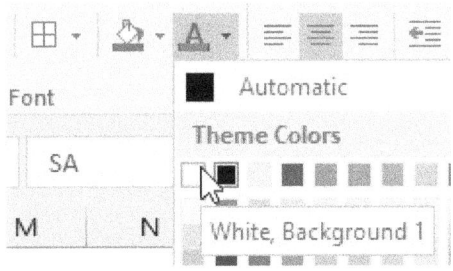

22. Configure the other cells like the image below

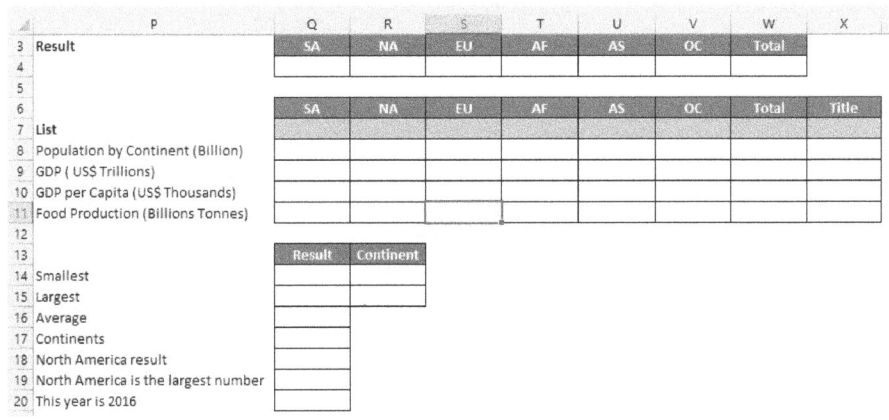

23. Use the "Gray -25%, Background 2, Darker 50%" color to make the ranges (A1:N25) look like the figure below.

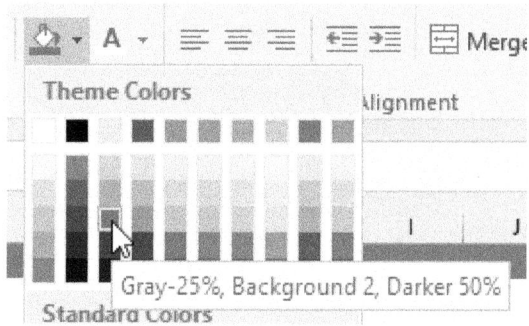

24. Select Range P3:P20 and go to the "Home Tab", "Alignment group" and then click on "Align Right".

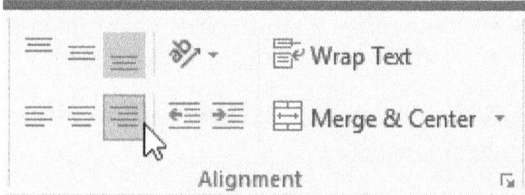

25. Click with the right button on cell Q3 and click "Insert Comment". Type South America and press "Tab".

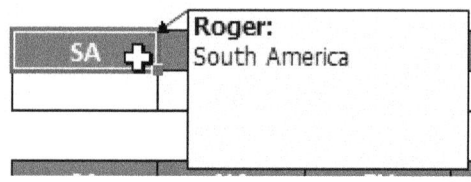

26. You will insert the following comments: cell R3 North America, cell S3 Europe, cell T3 Africa, cell U3 Asia and cell V3 Oceania.

27. Click on save, or press Ctrl+S to save your document

Congratulations! You have now created the tables and formatted your Spreadsheet!

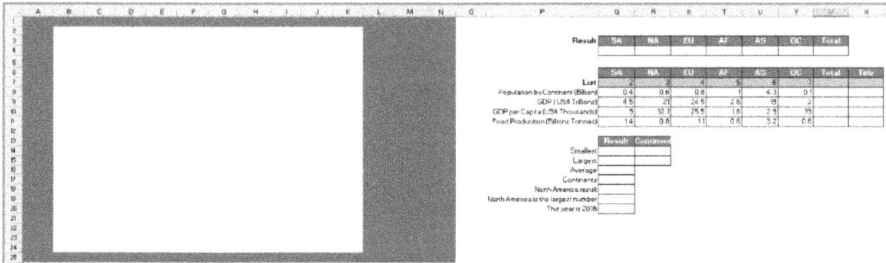

8. Dynamic Data

What gets measured gets managed.

- Peter Drucker, writer, professor, management consultant and self-described "social ecologist".

In this chapter you work with data validation and formulas including the famous VLOOKUP and HLOOKUP.

	3/04/2016							
Result	SA	NA	EU	AF	AS	OC	Total	
Population by Continent (Billion)	0.4	0.6	0.8	1	4.3	0.1	7.2	
	SA	NA	EU	AF	AS	OC	Total	Title
List	2	3	4	5	6	7	8	9
Population by Continent (Billion)	0.4	0.6	0.8	1	4.3	0.1	7.2	Total
GDP (US$ Trillions)	4.5	21	24.5	2.6	19	2	73.6	Total
GDP per Capita (US$ Thousands)	9	32.1	25.5	1.6	2.9	39	18.35	Avg
Food Production (Billions Tonnes)	1.4	0.8	1.1	0.6	3.2	0.6	7.7	Total

	Result	Continent
Smallest	0.1	OC
Largest	4.3	AS
Average	1.2	
Continents	6	
North America result	0.6	
North America is the largest number	FALSE	
This year is 2016	TRUE	

Example 2

28. Type =TODAY() in cell Q2 and press "Enter". It will return the current date.

29. Type information below into range Q7:X11.

	Q	R	S	T	U	V	W	X
6	SA	NA	EU	AF	AS	OC	Total	Title
7	2	3	4	5	6	7	8	9
8	0.4	0.6	0.8	1	4.3	0.1		Total
9	4.5	21	24.5	2.6	19	2		Total
10	9	32.1	25.5	1.6	2.9	39		Avg
11	1.4	0.8	1.1	0.6	3.2	0.6		Total

30. Type =SUM(Q8:V8) in cell W8 and press "Enter".

31. Select cell W9 and press "Crtl+d" to copy the information above.

32. Type =AVERAGE(Q10:V10) in cell W10 and press "Enter".

33. Type =SUM(Q11:V11) in cell W11 and press "Enter".

34. By this time your table must to look like the figure below.

	SA	NA	EU	AF	AS	OC	Total	Title
List	2	3	4	5	6	7	8	9
Population by Continent (Billion)	0.4	0.6	0.8	1	4.3	0.1	7.2	Total
GDP (US$ Trillions)	4.5	21	24.5	2.6	19	2	73.6	Total
GDP per Capita (US$ Thousands)	9	32.1	25.5	1.6	2.9	39	18.35	Avg
Food Production (Billions Tonnes)	1.4	0.8	1.1	0.6	3.2	0.6	7.7	Total

35. Select range C5:J5 and go to the "Home tab", "Alignment group" and then click on "Merge Across".

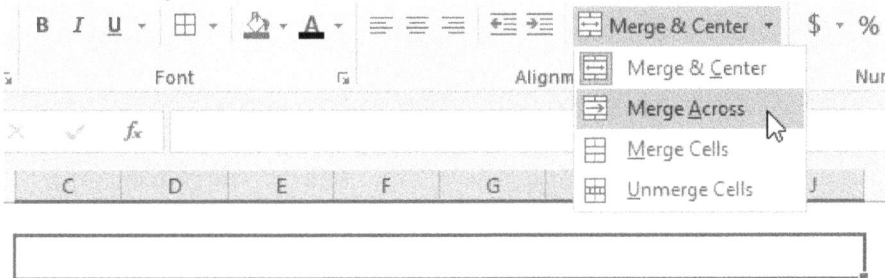

36. Select C5 and go to "Data tab", "Data Tools group" and click on "Data Validation".

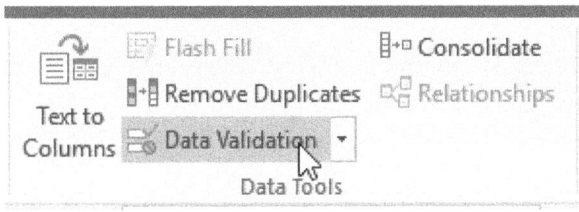

37. Go to Setting Option and set "Allow: List" and then type =P8:P11 on the field source.

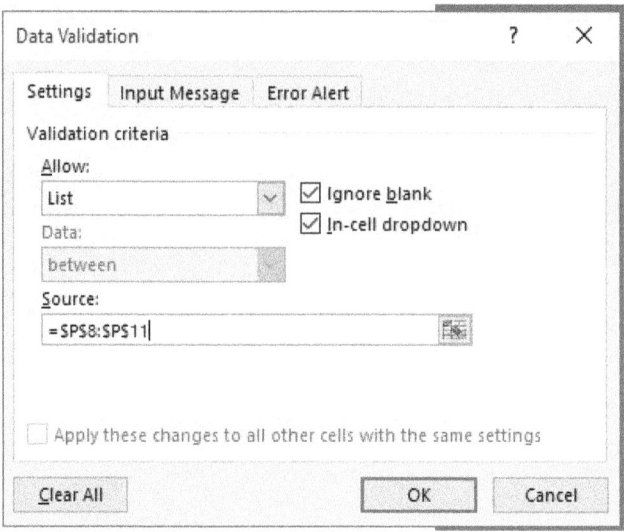

38. Range C5:J5 was configured to have a "List" with the values in the range P8:P11. Click and select the first option.

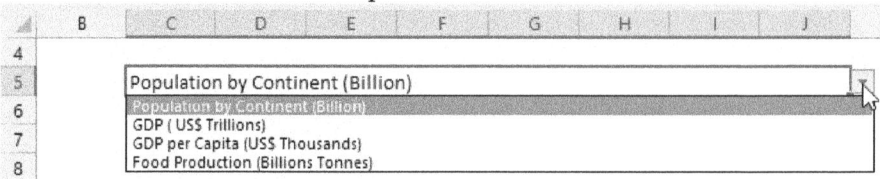

39. Type =C5 in cell P4 and press "Enter". Every time you change your list in cell C5, cell P4 will have the same text.

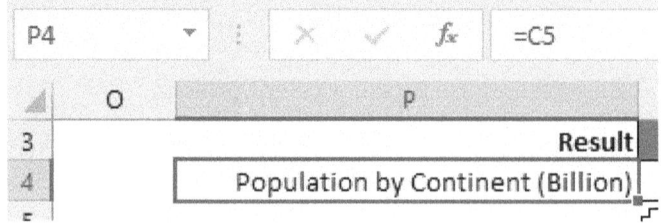

40. Now we will use the VLOOKUP function to bring data to range Q4:W4. The figure below will give you a brief explanation.

VLOOKUP - Vertical Lookup

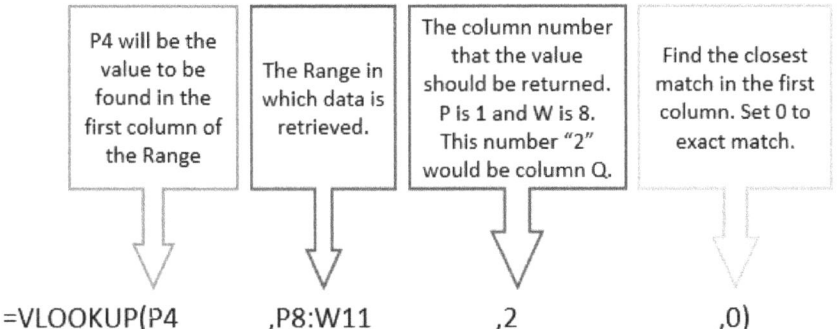

=VLOOKUP(P4   ,P8:W11   ,2   ,0)

VLOOKUP(lookup_value,table_array,col_index_num,range_lookup)
Looks for a value in the leftmost column of a table, and then returns a value in the same row from a column you specify. By default, the table must be sorted in an ascending order.

41. Type =VLOOKUP($P$4,$P$8:$W$11,Q7,0) in cell Q4

42. The $ sign is used to refer to a cell in a specific location or absolute reference. The "lookup_value" and the "table_array" (figure above) will always be the same.

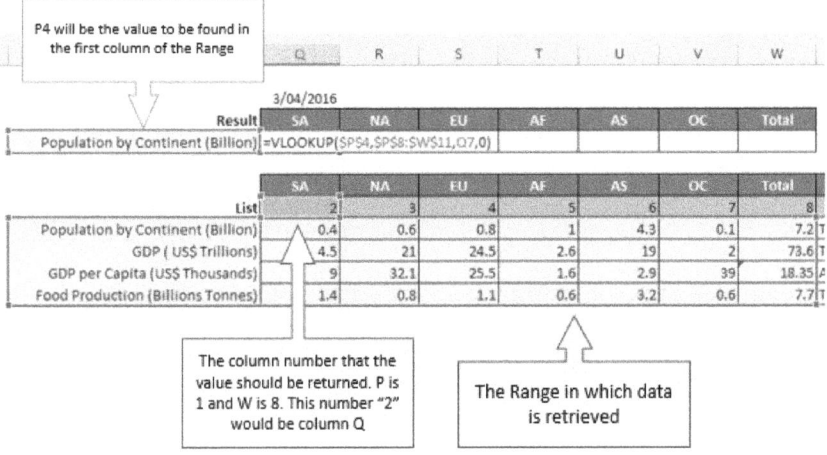

43. If you want, can use the insert function. Go to the "Home tab", "Editing group" and click in more functions. Select VLOOKUP and follow the steps (figure below).

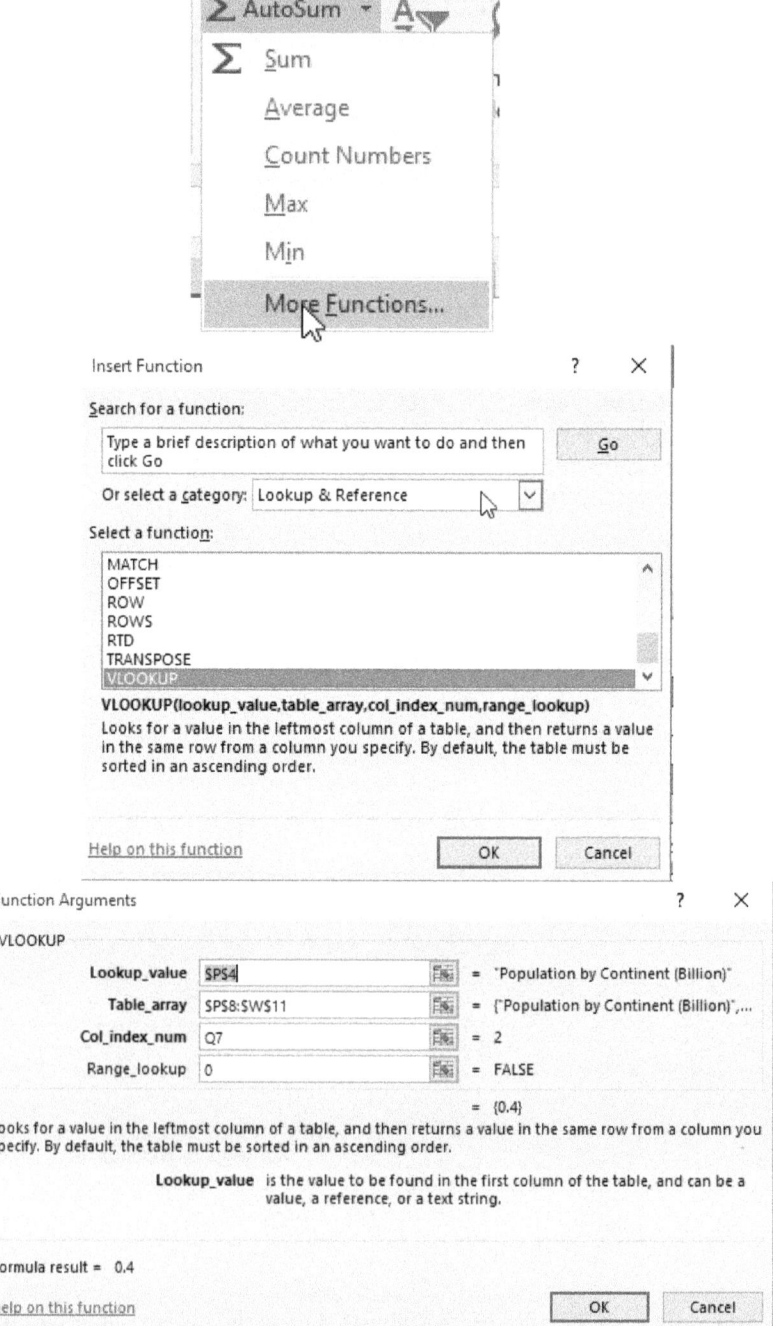

44. You will save your time by using the "Auto Fill" feature. Move your mouse to the little handle in the bottom-right corner of cell Q4, the mouse handle will turn into a black cross (see picture below).

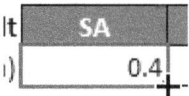

45. Click and drag to cell W4 and then release your mouse button.

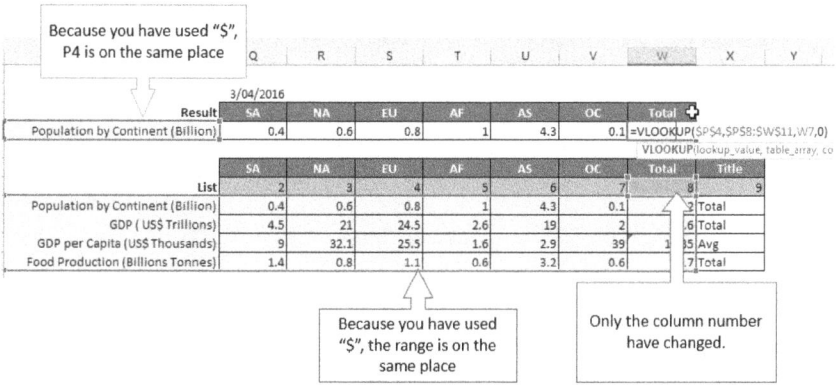

46. Select cell W4 and press the "F2" key. Note that only "column_index_number" have changed. Press "Esc".

47. Type =MIN(Q4:V4) in cell Q14 and press "Enter". Returns the smallest number.

48. Type =MAX(Q4:V4) in cell Q15 and press "Enter". Returns the largest number.

49. Type =AVERAGE(Q4:V4) in cell Q16 and press "Enter". Returns the average.

50. Type =COUNT(Q4:V4) in cell Q17 and press "Enter". Counts the number of cells that contain numbers.

51. Type =SUMIF(Q3:V4,"NA",Q4:V4) in cell Q18 and press "Enter". Sum the cells specified by a condition.

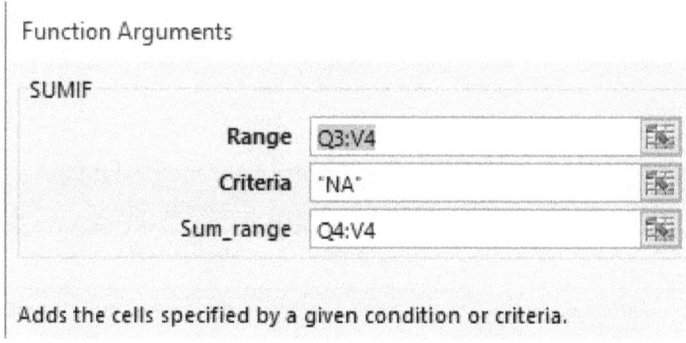

52. Type =Q18=Q15 in cell Q19 and press "Enter". Returns True or False (Q18 is equal to Q15).

53. Type =YEAR(Q2)=2016 in cell Q20 and press "Enter". Returns True or False (year of Q2 is equal to 2016).

54. Type =HLOOKUP(Q14,$Q$4:$W$6,3,0), in cell R14. Different from vlookup, HLOOKUP will look horizontally for value in the top of the row.

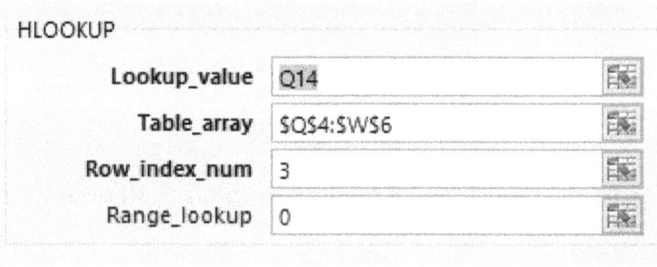

55. The figure below will give you the details of the formula.

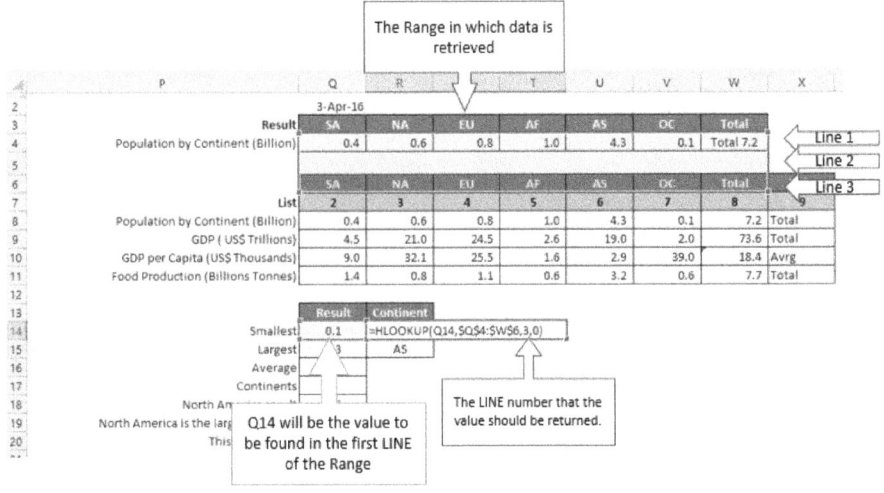

56. Select cell R15 and press "Crtl+D" to copy the cell above.

57. Select Range Q3:X20, go to the "Home tab", "Alignment group" and click on "Center".

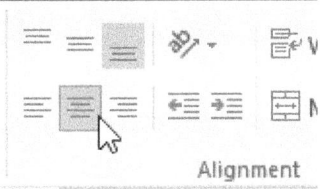

58. Click on save or press Ctrl+S to save your document.

Congratulations! You have now created the tables and formatted your Spreadsheet!

	3/04/2016						
Result	SA	NA	EU	AF	AS	OC	Total
Population by Continent (Billion)	0.4	0.6	0.8	1	4.3	0.1	7.2

	SA	NA	EU	AF	AS	OC	Total	Title
List	2	3	4	5	6	7	8	9
Population by Continent (Billion)	0.4	0.6	0.8	1	4.3	0.1	7.2	Total
GDP (US$ Trillions)	4.5	21	24.5	2.6	19	2	73.6	Total
GDP per Capita (US$ Thousands)	9	32.1	25.5	1.6	2.9	39	18.35	Avg
Food Production (Billions Tonnes)	1.4	0.8	1.1	0.6	3.2	0.6	7.7	Total

	Result	Continent
Smallest	0.1	OC
Largest	4.3	AS
Average	1.2	
Continents	6	
North America result	0.6	
North America is the largest number	FALSE	
This year is 2016	TRUE	

9. Charts and Objects

The world is one big data problem.

- Andrew McAfee.

In this chapter you will create charts, insert images and shapes to give life to your data, representing them visually and dynamically.

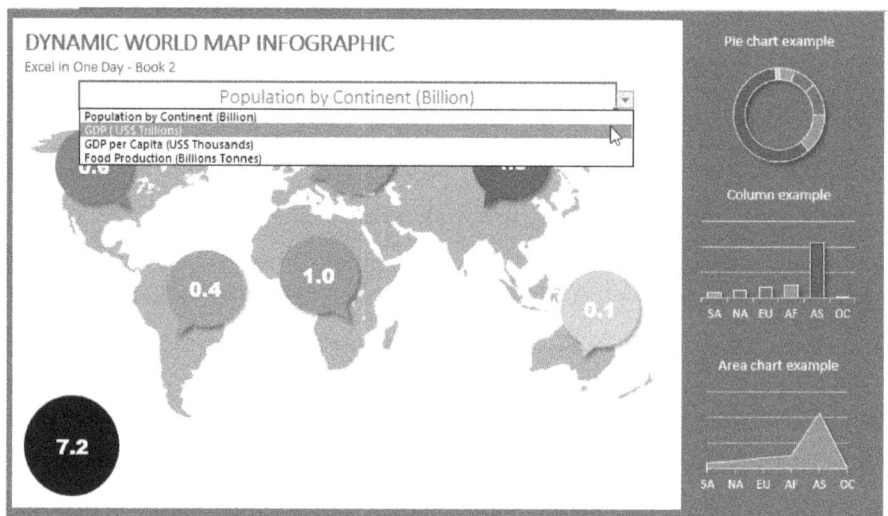

Example 3

59. Change the height to 6.00 in line 1 and line 25.

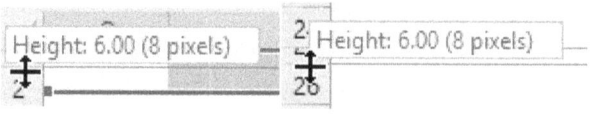

60. In column A, change the width to 0.50

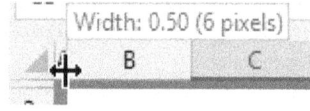

61. In cell C5, select font "Calibri Light", size "14", "Black, Text 1, Lighter 35%" color and "Center".

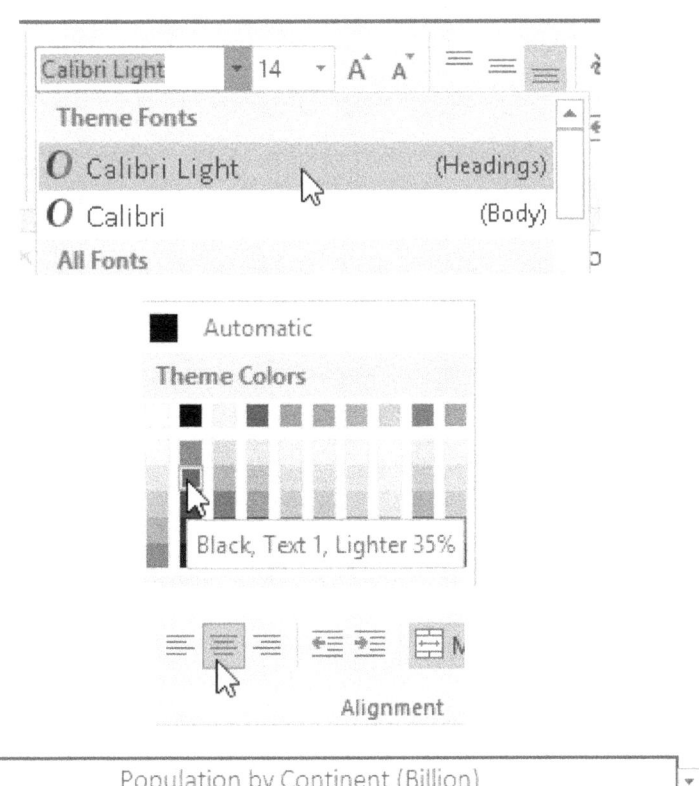

62. Go to "Insert tab", "Text group" and select "Text Box". Click in cell b2 to draw the text box and type DYNAMIC WORLD MAP INFOGRAPHIC Excel in One Day - Book 2. See figure below.

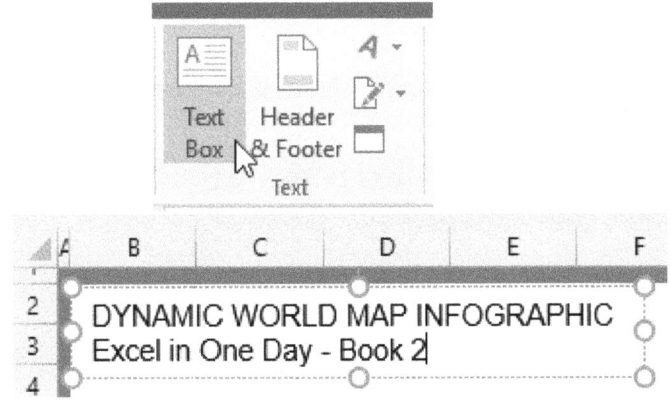

63. Select the first phrase and configure "Calibri Light", "Size 18", "Bold" and "Black, Text 1, Lighter 35%" color.

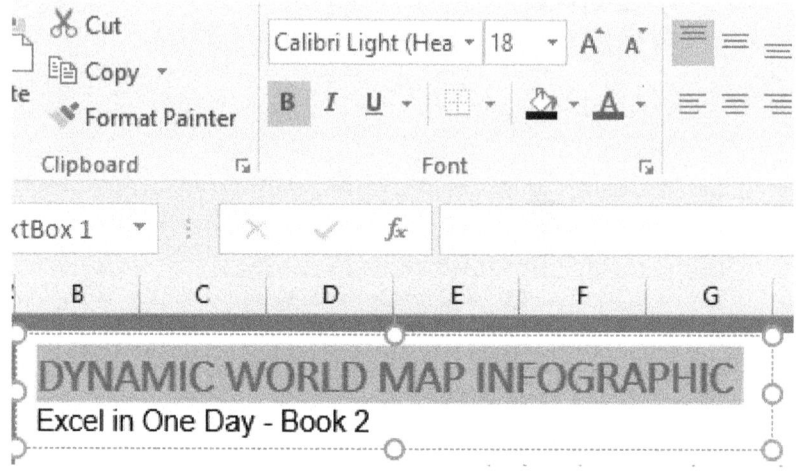

64. Select the second phrase and configure "Calibri Light", "Size 11" and "Black, Text 1, Lighter 35%" color.

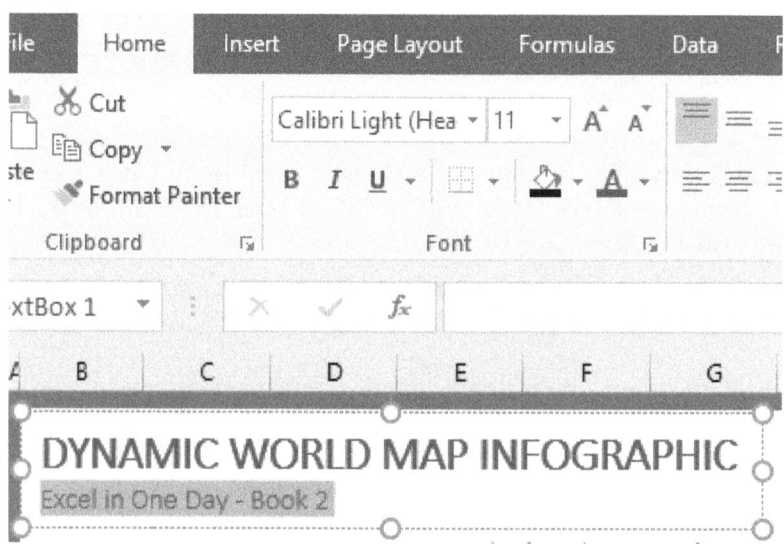

65. Go to http://rogerfsilva.blogspot.com/2017/06/books.html

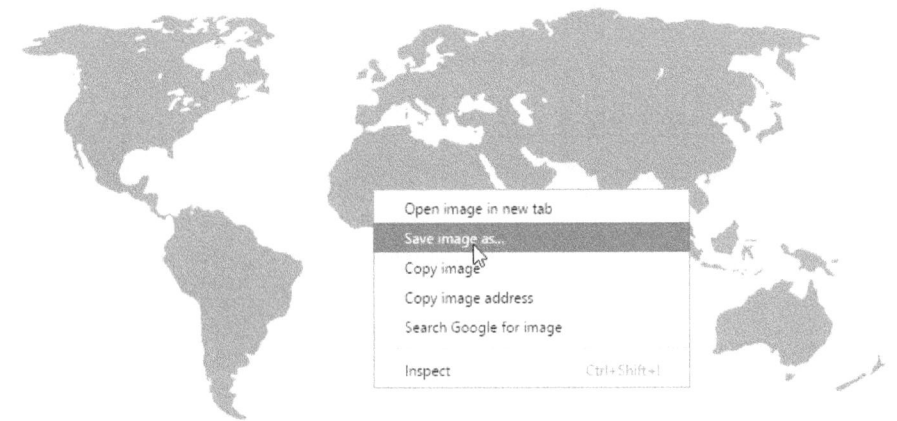

66. Download and save the file world_map.jpg in your desktop or any other location you choose.

67. Go to "Insert tab", "Illustrations group" and "Pictures". Find the world_map.jpg that you saved. Select and click "Enter".

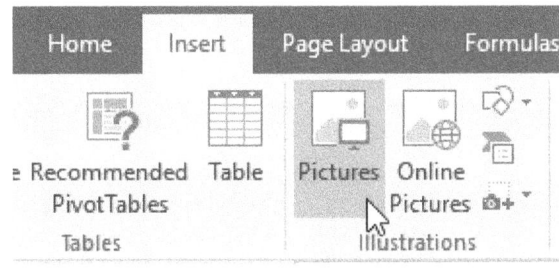

68. Click and drag the map and move close to cell B6.

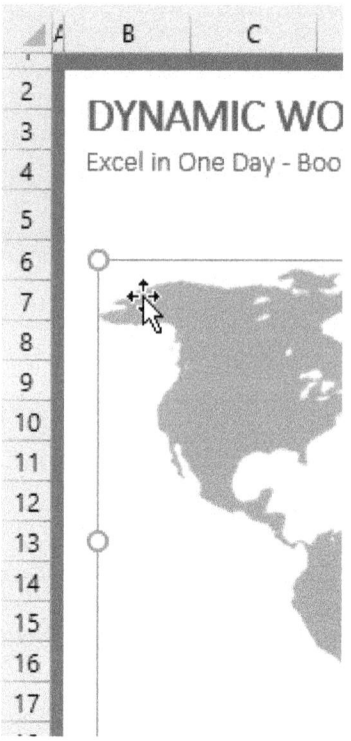

69. Go to "Format tab", "Size group", "Width" and type 16cm.

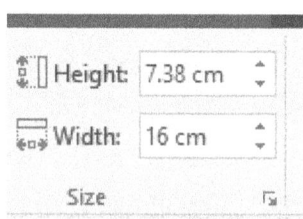

70. Go to "Insert tab", "Illustrations group", "Shapes" and select "Oval Callout".

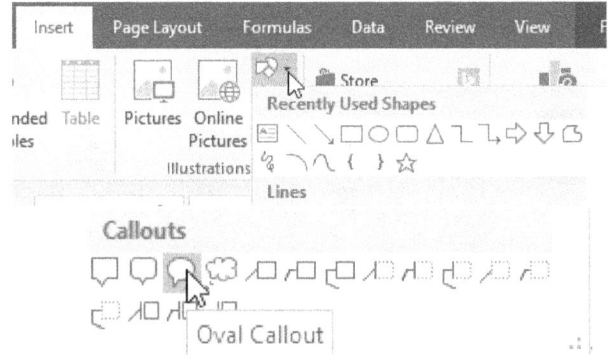

71. Click over the map to draw the shape. Go to "Format tab", "Size group", type 1.9cm for height and 2.0cm for width.

 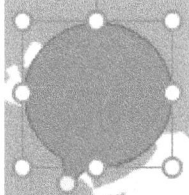

72. Go to "Tab format", "Shape outline" and select "No Outline".

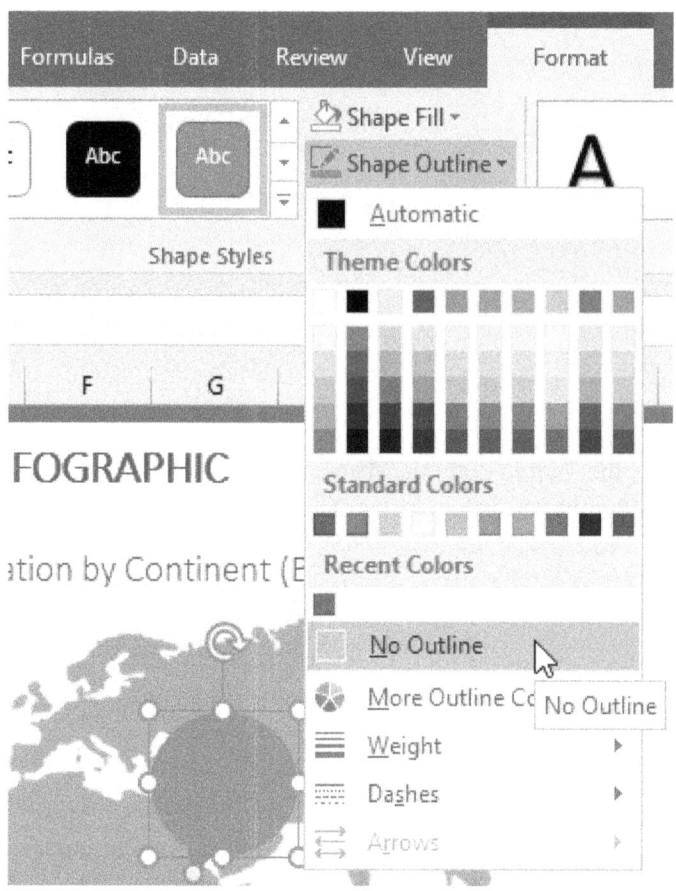

73. Go to "Shape Effects", "Shadow" and select "Offset Diagonal Bottom Right".

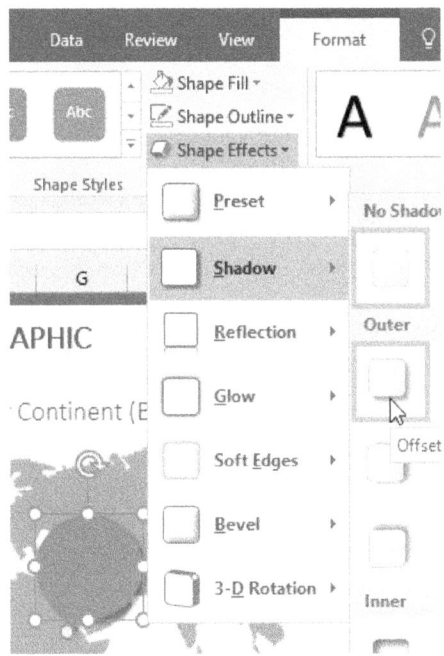

74. Click the right button and select "Format Shape". Go to "Format Shape box", "Text Options", "Text Box" and type in "Left margin" 0.1 cm and in "Right margin" 0.1 cm.

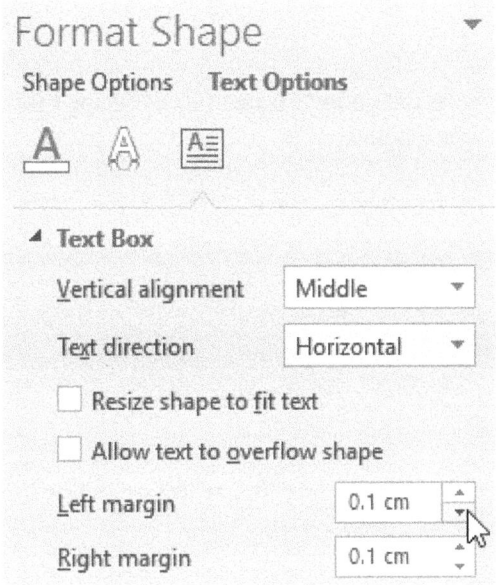

75. Select the shape and then "Copy" and "Paste" five times to have six shapes in total.

76. Drag the shapes over each continent.

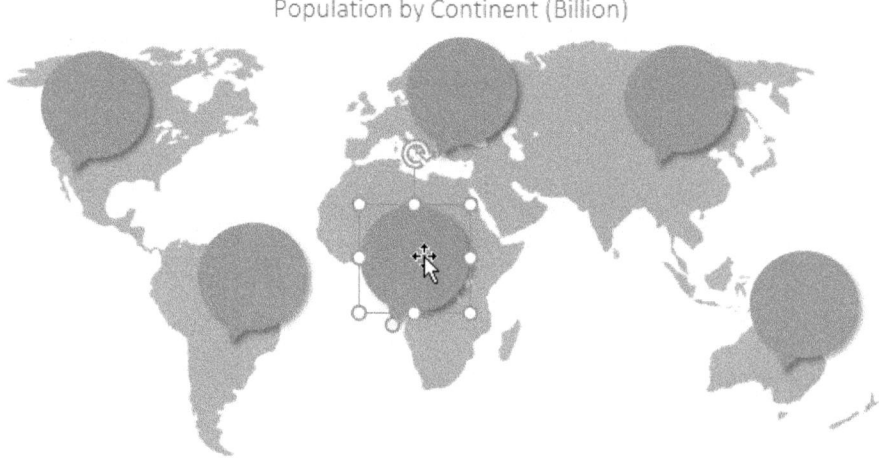

77. With the shape selected go to "Format tab", "Shape Fill" and select the colors to match the figure below.

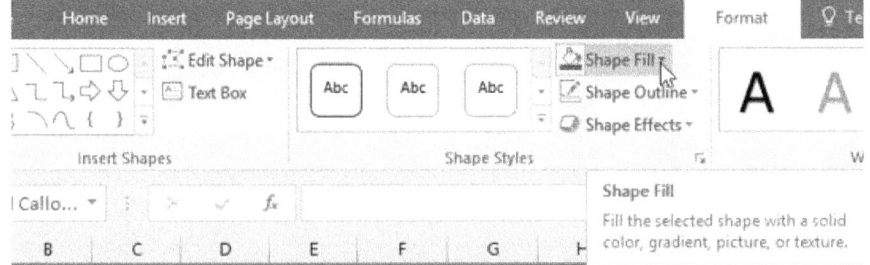

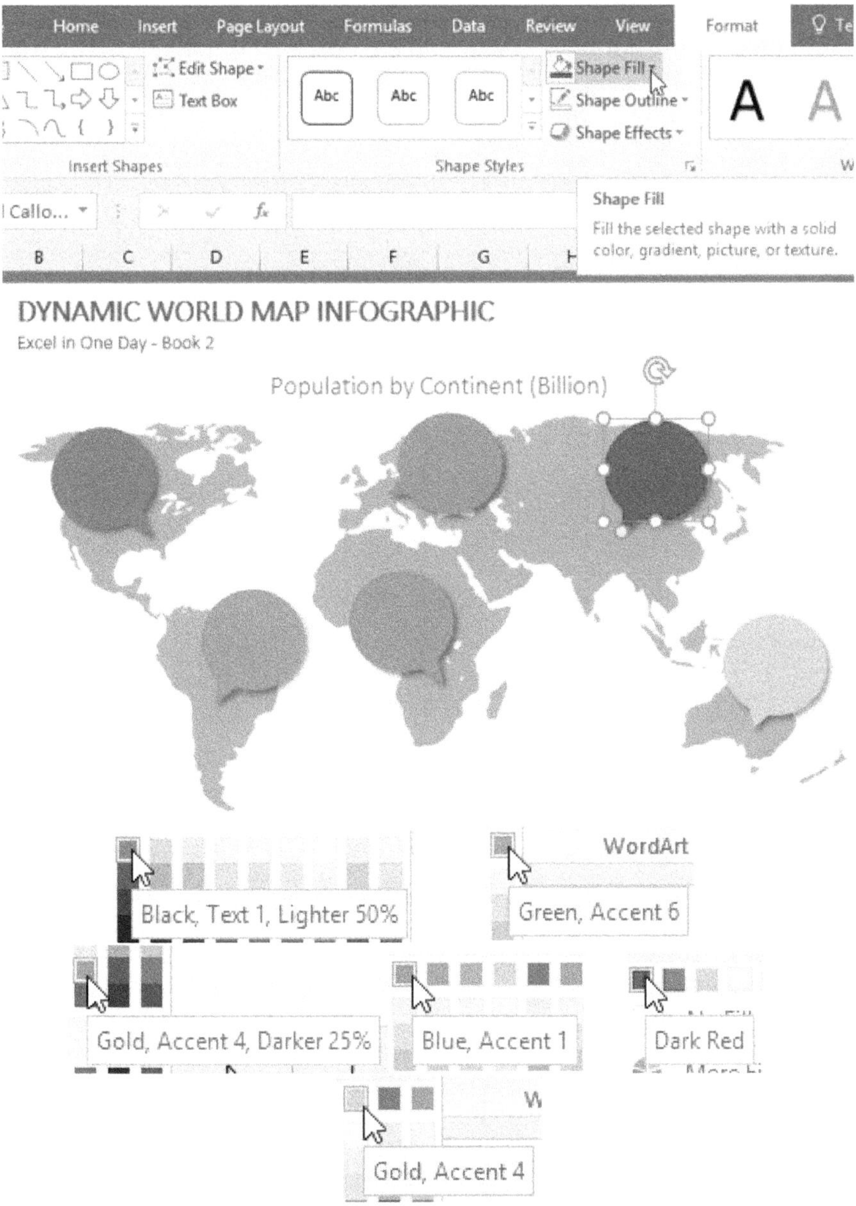

78. Edit the shapes (left or right) by dragging the handle.

79. Select the "North America" shape and type =R4 in Formula Bar. The NA value will be set in the shape.

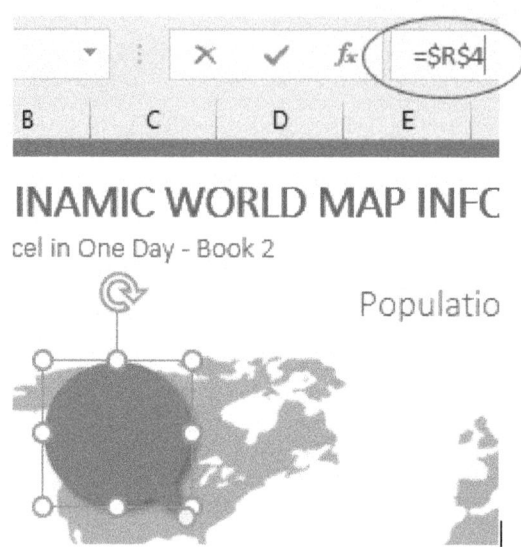

80. Repeat this for the other shapes: SA =Q4, EU =S4, AF =T4, AS =U4 and OC =V4.

81. Select the Shapes, go to "Home tab", and select "Arial Black" font, "Size" 14, "White, Background 1" font color, "Center" and "Middle Align".

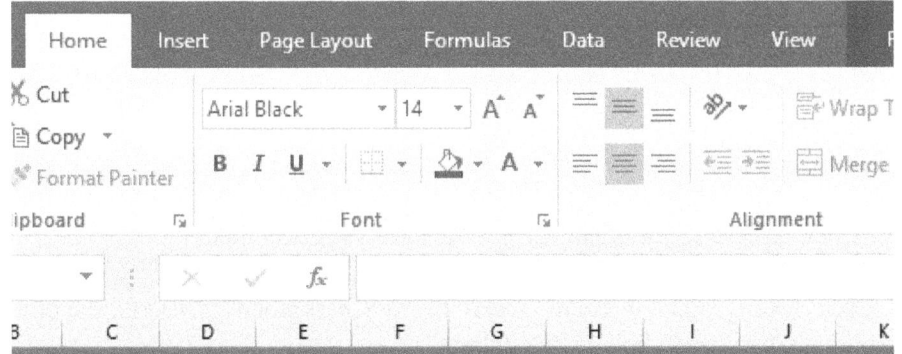

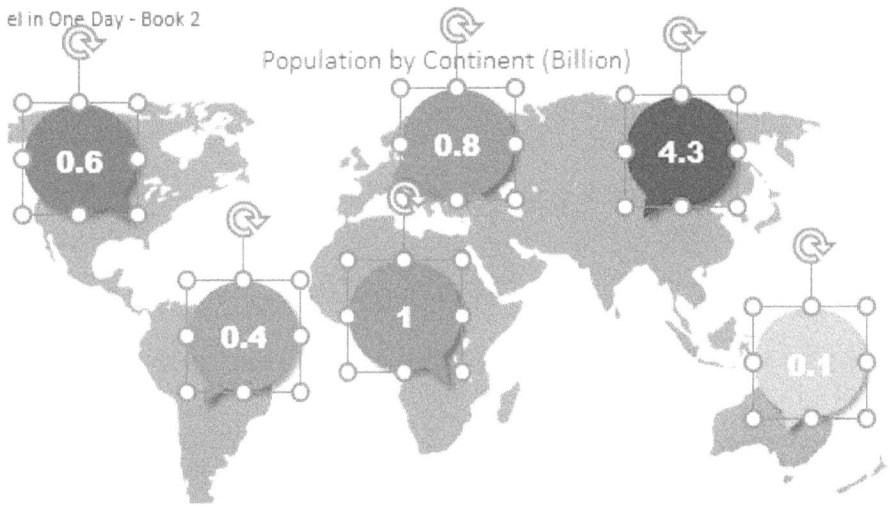

82. Now Create (same as image below):

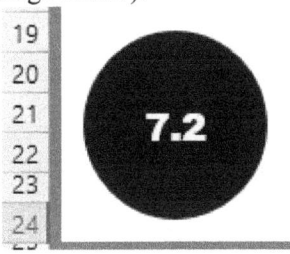

a. Oval Shape.
b. Drag close to cell B19
c. Set the value: =W4
d. Shape Height: 2.5.
e. Shape Width: 2.5.
f. Shape Fill: Gray -25%, Background 2, Darker 90%.
g. Shape Outline: No outline.

h. Font: Arial Black.
i. Size: 14.
j. Font Color: White.
k. Center.
l. Middle Align.

83. Click on "Save", or press "Ctrl+S" to save your document.

84. Select Range Q3:V4. Go to "Insert Tab", "Chart group", "Insert a Pie or a Doughnut Chart" and click on "Doughnut".

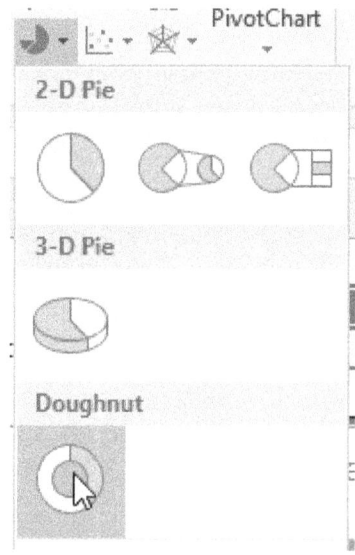

85. Click on "Chart Title" and type Pie chart example.

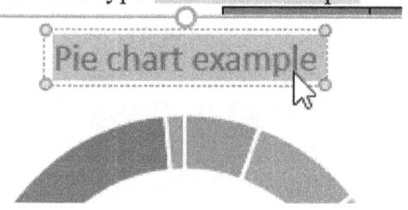

86. Double click the "Point" "AS", go to "Format tab", "Shape Fill" and select the same color to match the one on the map (Dark Red). Do the same process to every "Series Point".

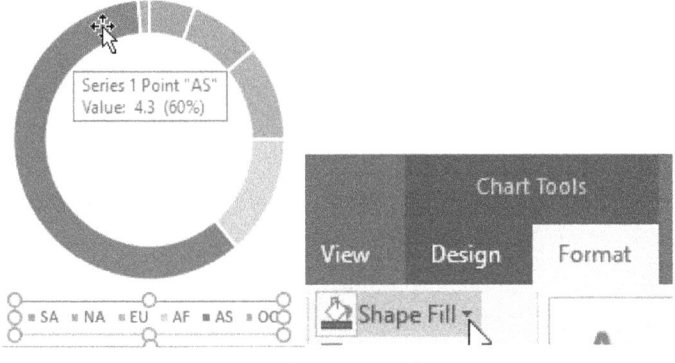

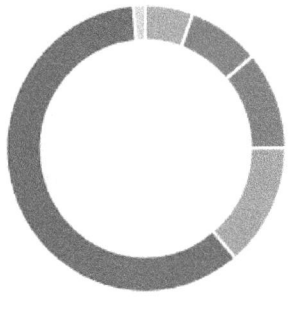

87. Double Click on "Chart Legend" and press "Delete".

88. Go to "Format tab", "Size group" and type "Height" 3.9 and Width 4.3.

89. Double click on the Chart title, select the text and go to "Home tab", "Font Size" and select 11.

90. Drag the chart close to cell L2.

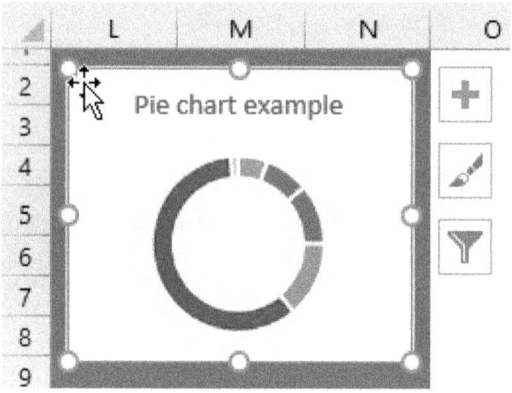

91. Go to "Format tab", "Shape Fill" and select "No Fill".

92. Go to "Format tab", "Shape Outline" and select "No Outline".

93. Change the chart title to white.

94. Go to "Format tab", "Current Selection" and select "Series 1"

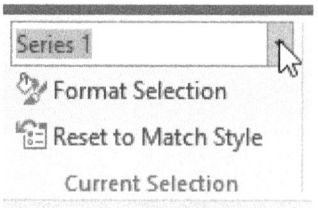

95. Go to "Format tab", "Shape Effects", "Shadow" and select "Offset Diagonal Bottom Right".

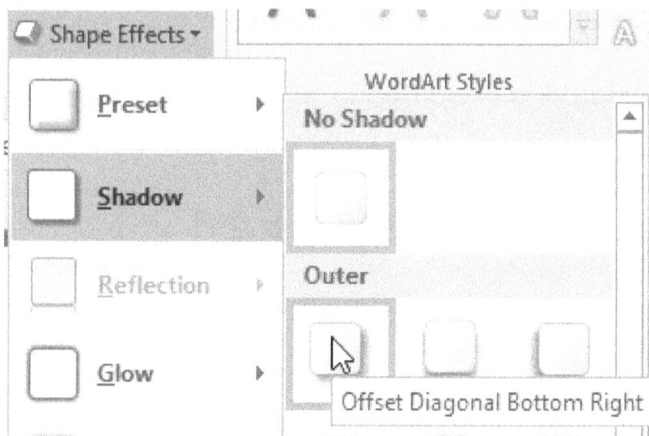

96. Go to "Shape Effects", "Shadow" and select "Offset Diagonal Bottom Right".

97. With "Series 1" selected go to "Format tab", "Shape Outline", "Weight" and 1pt.

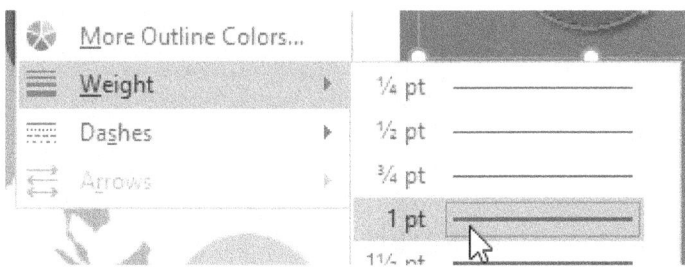

98. Select the Chart and "Copy". Click in cell L9 and "Paste". Click in cell L17 and "Paste" again.

99. Hold "Crtl" and select the three charts. Go to "Format tab", "Arrange group", "Align" and select "Align Center".

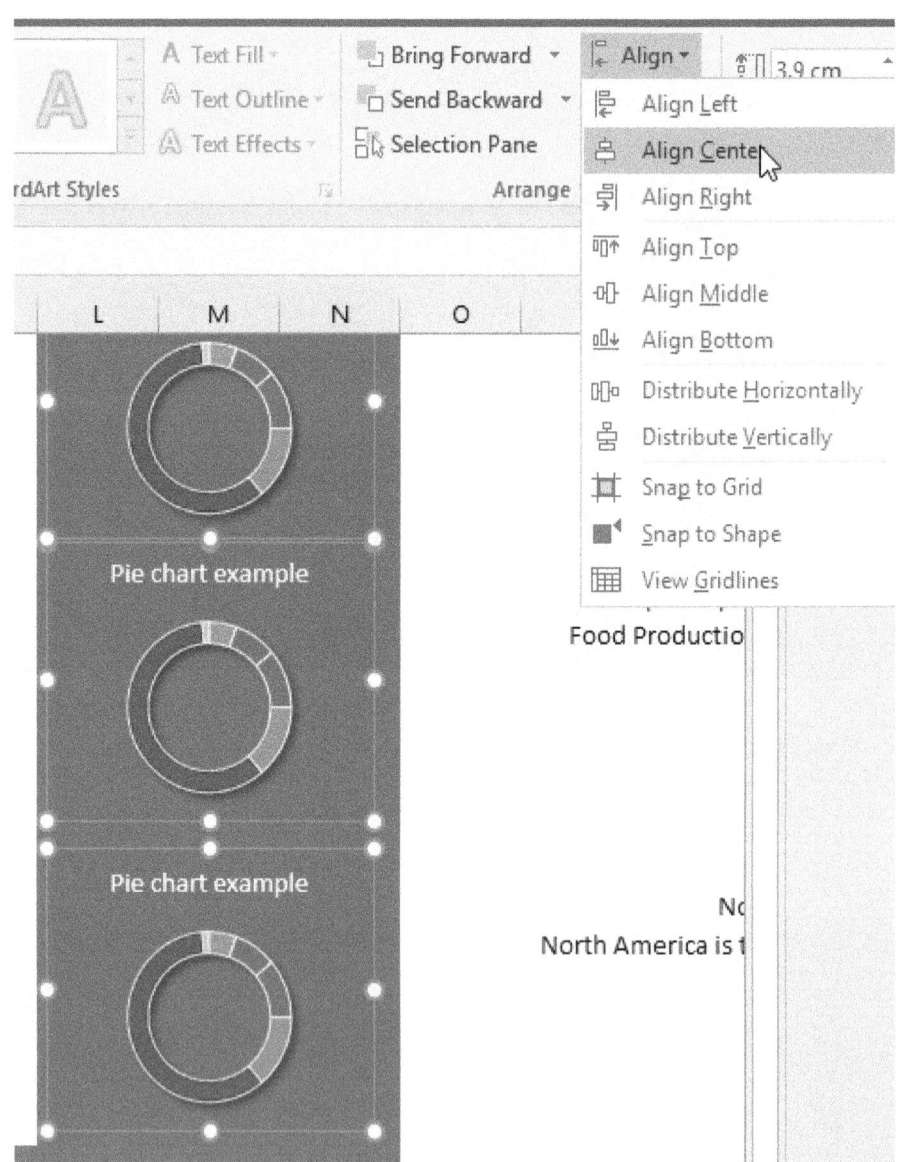

100. Select the second chart and Go to "Design tab", "Type group", "Change Chart Type", "Column" and select 'Clustered Column".

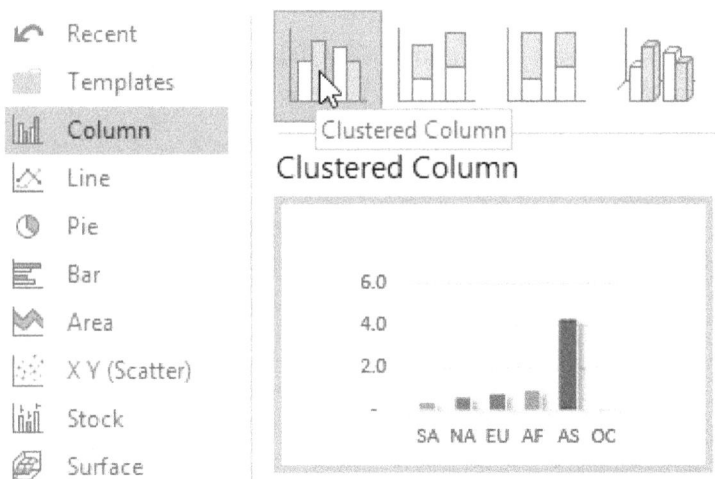

101. Select "Vertical (Value) Axis" and "Delete".

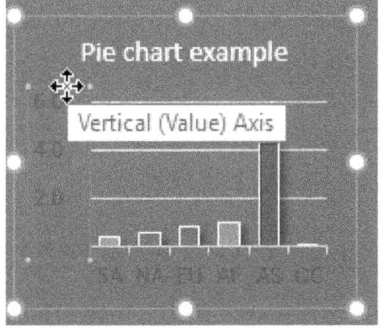

102. Select "Horizontal (Category) Axis", go to "Font Color" and select white. Change the "Chart Title" to Column example.

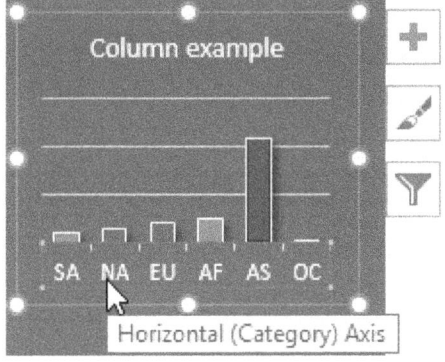

103. Select the third chart and Go to "Design tab", "Type group", "Change Chart Type", "Column" and select 'Clustered Column".

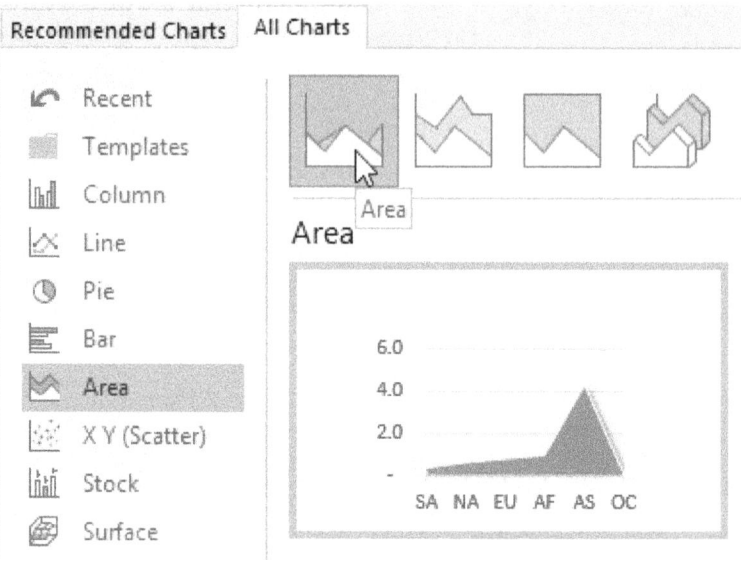

104. Select "Vertical (Value) Axis" and "Delete".

105. Select "Horizontal (Category) Axis", go to "Font Color" and select white color. Change the "Chart Title" to Area chart example.

106. Select Range Q4:W4 go to "Home tab", "Number group", increase and decrease decimals to have only one decimal.

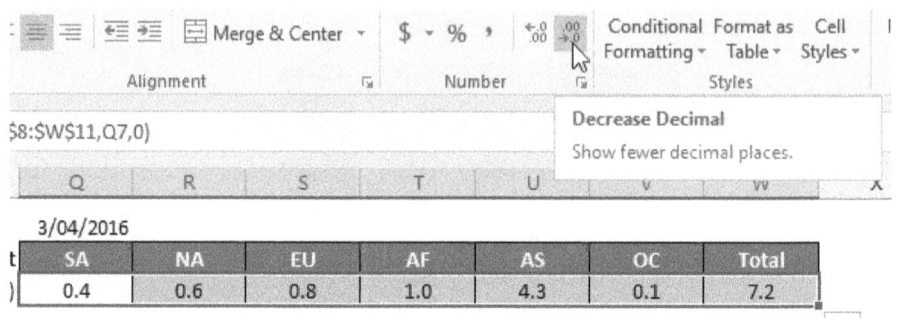

107. Click on "Save" or press "Ctrl+S" to save your document.

Congratulations! You have now finished your Dynamic Infographic!

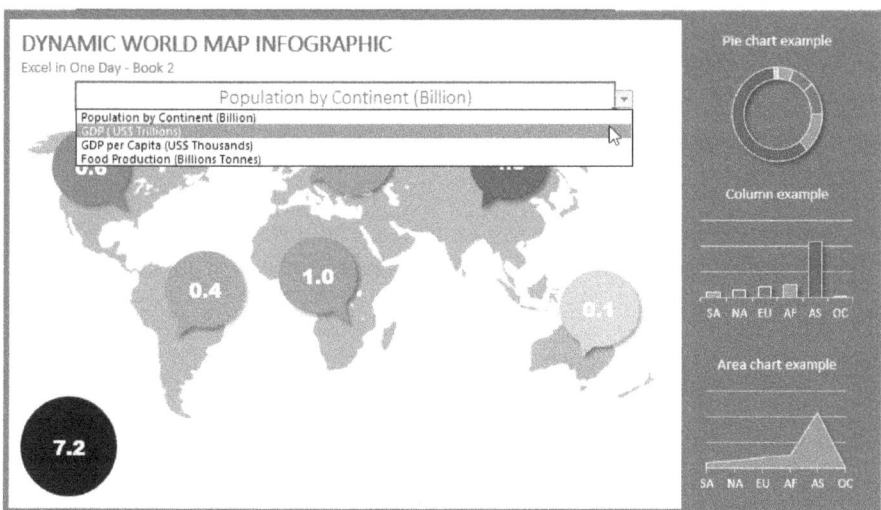

Dear reader.

A good rating and your positive review are incredibly important for me! If you have any comments or suggestion, please send me an email, or a message on LinkedIn and I will be more than happy to hear from you.

☆☆☆☆☆

I hope you have achieved your goal to learn more about Microsoft Excel quickly and creating a beautiful and useful tool.

For its constant evolution, try my other books in the Create and Learn series and go evolving rapidly, create new tools and learn new practices in Microsoft Excel.

Thank you for the time we spent Creating and Learning.

Roger F. Silva

rogerfsilva1@gmail.com

You can find more Create and Learn books at http://rogerfsilva.blogspot.com

Lightning Source UK Ltd.
Milton Keynes UK
UKHW012221210220
359132UK00001B/141